The T-Shirt Revolution

Building Your Business Using a Digital Apparel Printer

Chase Roh, Ph.D.

AND

David A. Lavita

Amboss Publishing

The T-shirt Revolution
Building Your Business Using
a Digital Apparel Printer

Amboss Publishing

Copyright ©2008 by Amboss Publishing
Published by Amboss Publishing

ISBN: 978-0-615-25091-5

Printed in the United States of America

Visit www.t-shirtbook.com
for updates and additional material.

This book is dedicated to
Dee Roh and Karen LaVita.
Without their sacrifices and encouragement,
we never would have found the time to write it.

Contents

Preface

This book is written for the benefit of screen printers, embroiders, and other garment decorators who are interested in digital apparel printing using inkjet technology. We have seen a great number of entrepreneurs entering the garment decoration industry thanks to this emerging technology. Thus, we also devoted a part of the book to give an overview of the industry. This may be also beneficial to those who are already in garment decoration. There are vastly different operational characteristics and economics at play with direct-to-garment printers compared to traditional screen printing. Thus, garment decorators will have to adjust their business model when they adopt direct-to-garment printers. We devoted a significant section to sales and marketing to show how decorators can best utilize new digital printers to enhance their business. Finally, we added a chapter about the promotional wear industry, which is the fastest-growing sector of the decorated garment industry.

Although we frequently use the term "digital apparel printer," we are really referring to specifically the so-called "direct-to-garment" printer —an inkjet printer that prints graphics *directly* onto the garments and other substrates like mouse pads, typically using water-based pigmented inks. In essence, this technology is the future of the garment decoration industry; we expect most garment printers will switch to direct-to-garment printing over the next twenty years for reasons of performance, costs and environmental consideration. Some people use the term "direct-to-garment" printing to distinguish from earlier attempts to use (dye sublimation) inkjet or laser printers — both digital printers – to print images on a transfer sheet which will be applied to garments with heat. Although practiced in specialty shops and by hobbyists in the past, such methods lacked the technical or commercial merits needed to be widely adopted for commercial garment decoration. As we will discuss in detail, such non-direct-to-garment digital printing is in decline. When we say "digital apparel printer" or "digital printer" in this book, the terms are interchangeable with "direct-to-garment printer."

This book is an outgrowth of our interactions with many folks in the garment decoration industry. We both have occasionally participated in the distributor training sessions at AnaJet, and some of the materials were developed for presentation at those seminars. As the company grew, we both largely moved on from the training programs — but our interest and fascination in this burgeoning industry continues. According to a 2007 industry study by *Impressions* magazine, it is a $44-billion business (wholesale value), conducted by 55,000 entities in the U.S. Since we estimate the value added by garment decorators is about 60%, the garment decoration is indeed a fairly large industry. A market research firm, I.T. Strategies, estimates the world-wide market retail value of decorated apparel is as much as $121 billion. This gives an idea on the magnitude and importance of this industry.

The two primary traditional methods of decorating garments are screen printing and embroidery. Commercial embroidery went through the "digital revolution" more than twenty years ago. Although a digital method of screen preparation has been developed, today's screen printing process is pretty much as it has been for hundreds of years. We believe direct-to-garment printing technology is the key to the digital revolution of garment printing. Economics aside, one of the most troublesome parts of screen printing is the plastisol ink, which contains PVC and phthalates. These are some of the most environmentally damaging materials made by man, and phthalates used as plasticizer is highly carcinogenic. Efforts to develop more environmentally-friendly screen printing ink have not been very successful. We believe that digital printing's gradual replacement of screen printing with more environmentally-friendly water-based digital ink will be good for the environment. But the driving force of the change will be economics.

Direct-to-garment printing technology is still evolving. During its short existence, some early entrants have over-sold and hyped the technology. Many in the industry are concerned about its future. We will soon see a shakeout of the industry, and then it will move on to the next level. The key to success is customer education and full disclosure of any limitations by the manufacturers. Nothing can be more important than good customer education and continuous technical support regarding this technology. As of this writing, those purpose-built textile printers perform well if they are maintained properly. It is our hope that this book can contribute to the education of and about the industry.

For proper disclosure, we should mention that we are co-founders and officers of AnaJet, a manufacturer of direct-to-garment printers. We made every effort not to let this book be an extension of our day job, but rather to be a balanced reference guide for the industry. We limited mention of the AnaJet experience as best we could, and fairly presented all products in the market. But on a few occasions we were obliged to mention AnaJet brand names, such as ARTprint™ and PHOTOshirts™ as there were no generic equivalents; AnaJet is the only maker offering such products. You, the reader, will be the final judge how well we have done in making an unbiased presentation. We should also mention that Melco Embroidery System, a division of the huge Swiss corporation Oerlikon, is a private brand customer of AnaJet for the MelcoJet printer. We discuss the MelcoDirector production management program and Melco LiveDesign program, as we are just familiar with these products — and frankly, they are among the best products in the industry.

We are indebted to many people in writing this book. Although we cannot list all those who have contributed to our efforts, we wish to acknowledge the following reviewers. Johnny Shell, SGIA Vice President for Technical Services, has reviewed and commented on parts of the manuscript. Patti Williams of I.T. Strategies also reviewed some chapters and provided valuable advice. Our good friend Dr. Franz Bosshard — CEO of the world's third-largest appliance manufacturer, BSH Home Appliances, and marketer par excellence — reviewed the sales and marketing chapters. Dr. L. W. Gertmenian, Distinguished Professor of Economics at Pepperdine University, also provided valuable advice on economic subjects and presentation of the material. Our acknowledgements do not imply that the above reviewers agree with our views. Of course, any remaining errors and biases are entirely the fault of the authors.

We are most grateful for the five direct-to-garment business operators who are featured in our success stories in Chapter Four. They sacrificed their privacy and revealed some of their business practices to help other direct-to-garment printers and advance the industry. We are also indebted to some of our colleagues at AnaJet. Among them, Edward Joseph contributed to the mixed media decoration section. Paul Green provided advice regarding graphic preparation for direct-to-garment printing, and also prepared most of the charts and graphics that appear in this book.

We would also like to thank several organizations that generously gave us permission to use their survey results and research analyses. *Impressions* magazine's 2007 Decorated Apparel Industry Universe Study was indispensable for providing a grasp of the industry. So were the studies by I.T. Strategies. We also used studies by SGIA, ASI and PPAI. Whenever possible, we provided proper credit in the text or Endnotes. The Endnotes also contain the bibliography.

Finally we would like to thank our wives, Dee Roh and Karen LaVita, to whom this book is dedicated. We had to write and refine this book entirely while in airplanes and on evenings and weekends, as we have day jobs. During this period, our wives had to live and run households largely without our help. Dee, being in this business, read most of the chapters and made many valuable suggestions to improve the presentation.

Chase Roh
David A. LaVita

August 24, 2008

CHAPTER 1

Will Your Business Be a Start-up?

I f you are thinking of adding direct-to-garment printing to your existing business, this chapter is not for you. Go directly to Chapter Two. But if your business will be a start-up, read on. In this chapter, we will discuss why owning a small business is so appealing in today's economy and what kind of opportunities digital apparel printers can provide you.

LOOKING OUT FOR YOURSELF

Not so long ago, young Americans typically dreamed of working their way up in large, prestigious corporations like IBM, Digital Equipment, Kodak or General Motors. Most expected employment with these companies to last a lifetime, ending in a happy retirement with health care and a pension provided by the benevolent employer. But things have changed drastically since the 1990s.

Technological innovations fueled by the Internet, Y2K projects, new-age information systems and globalization have transformed businesses and society. Corporate mergers, reorganizations, computer-driven automation and competition from low-cost overseas manufacturers created massive layoffs. Many are trying to reduce retirees' health care benefits. Governments also find it increasingly difficult to provide effective leadership to the business communities and the societies. We can no longer be sure that even the Social Security system will take care of our needs in old age. Nationhood seems to be giving way to individual sovereignty.[1] Ordinary folks can no longer rely on either their "corporate mothers" or the government.

Thanks to the rise of personal computers, the once-thriving minicomputer industry disappeared virtually overnight, taking with it big companies like Digital, Data General and Centronics. With the advent of digital photography, photo finishing businesses have also declined rapidly. Kodak has become a much smaller and wounded company. Polaroid, once one of the most celebrated companies in the world, now exists only as an administrative shell after filing for bankruptcy in 2001. As consumer preferences shift to foreign-made cars, jobs at General Motors and other U.S. carmakers continue to shrink. Today, although GM is still the largest manufacturing company in the world, frequent reports of plant closings do not fuel confidence in job security there.

Yes, many large corporate businesses are still thriving. Such prosperity, however, no longer automatically trickles down to their employees. For better or worse, a place of work has become simply a place to work — you discharge your duties efficiently and receive fair wages. There is little corporate loyalty now. You must be prepared to fend for yourself when adverse developments appear.

Individuals have to become financially independent in their own ways.[1,2] The popular financial educator and motivational speaker Robert Kiyosaki of *Rich Dad, Poor Dad* fame has helped countless Americans in this regard. He emphasizes that one should own a business, however small it may be.[3] When you work for an employer, you have a job; but when you are self-employed, like a lawyer or a consultant, you own your job. If you own a business, you have a system that works for you. If you are an investor, you make your money work for you. Still, holding a job is not a bad idea if you choose your profession carefully and you are successful at it.

Many centi-millionaires and deca-millionaires are corporate managers.[4] You have probably read many news reports about CEOs and CFOs who make hundreds of millions of dollars, and get astronomical amounts of severance pay – even when they are fired for doing a bad job. Unreported, of course, are the countless ordinary corporate managers who quietly take home more than a million dollars a year. However, most of us do not have the training, luck or experience to land those dream jobs.

The thought of being an investor and having your dollars work for you while you sleep or vacation in the South Seas is certainly nice. However, that kind of investing takes substantial capital to begin with, which most people do not have. The realistic best option for most will be to become self-employed or own your own business. The American dream is no longer just about owning a home, but about owning a business of your own. It does not matter if the business is small, as "a bit of something" has the potential to grow.

Those who run small businesses —defined as 500 employees or less — have good reason to be proud, as their combined contribution to the U.S. economy is greater than that of big businesses. According to SBA 2007 "Report to the President – The Small Business Economy," small businesses in 2004 accounted for all new net job creation. Small firms had a net gain of 1.86 million new jobs, while large firms lost 181,000 jobs.[5] Small businesses employed slightly more than half of all the private sector workforce and account for 50.7% of the non-farm private gross domestic product. A member of the median range of small businesses typically has one location with just four employees. As you will see in Chapter Six, home-based businesses are very important; they account for half of all U.S. businesses, and 36% of the decorated apparel industry.

The day you start a home-based garment decoration business, you are in the mainstream of the decorated apparel industry. When you hire three people, your business is the median of all American small businesses. No one should attach a stigma to a small start-up business. Although we cannot cite any reliable statistics, we learned from our European colleagues that a large percentage of UK and German garment decorators also are small or home-based businesses.

LOOKING FOR BUSINESS OPPORTUNITIES

It is, however, no easy matter to quit a corporate job suddenly and start a business of your own. We know, because we made this transition ourselves some years ago. Once you decide to start a business, you will find no shortage of opportunities offered at industry trade shows and in advertisements in business opportunity magazines. The problem is that there are too many choices, which can be confusing. It is important to sort out a gem from a snake oil salesman's pitch.

Since the franchise industry is now regulated heavily in the United States, buying into a reputable franchise operation can be a good option. Some franchise operators have developed proven operational procedures and will help with marketing. However, such benefits come at steep prices. Moreover, there are also many franchise operations that do not pan out as described in the fancy brochures and sales presentations. Today, a decent franchise with a good track record sells for upward of $200,000. A fast food franchise goes for half a million dollars, a quick printing shop goes for $250,000 or more, and a mailing center will cost you $150,000. But even at this level of investment, nothing is guaranteed.

Non-franchised business opportunities also abound; they range from distributorships to multilevel marketing, business coaches, seminar packages, equipment manufacturers, and business service group memberships. The possibility of misrepresentation and outright fraud also abounds. However, non-franchised businesses are generally more affordable. Hidden gems are rare. Finding one requires that you do your well-informed homework. There are many ways to approach business opportunities; we suggest the process below.

The first step is to **analyze yourself**. You must be highly motivated and willing to surmount any number of hurdles to achieve financial independence. You must be a self-starter who is unafraid of trying new things. If you are more comfortable following set procedures, you may be better off staying in your current job and aiming to become the company's future CEO. It is equally important that you have the **support of your family**. Running a business of your own consumes time and energy. Talk with your spouse and family and get their solid support behind you.

Next, you need to see whether a **particular opportunity suits you**. An opportunity that suits Peter well may not be the right one for Paul. A shy person who does not like to meet new people may not do well with a conventional small business. The small business owner is usually the "chief salesperson." He or she may not be at the forefront of sales activities at all times, but must take an active interest in sales and enjoy meeting customers.

A business model that is completely Internet-based may be better suited for a person who doesn't fit that description.

In the third step, ask yourself this question: What kind of opportunities will be the most attractive and financially sensible for you?

- **Low capital investment or Ten-Bagger Rule:** You are starting a small business and you do not want or cannot afford to invest a large sum of capital into it. Yet all of your efforts are meaningless if the small investment limits the potential growth of your business. The business must have a very high potential compared to a relatively low level of investment. This Ten-Bagger Rule will be explained further in a minute. Then you will not care for a rental business, which ties up substantial capital, or any other business requiring a large investment.
- **Easy-to-operate business:** Overly complex business models do not work for small businesses. You do not have the resources to hire managers who can handle complex issues.
- **High profit margin**: They may not be easy to find, but high margins are the only way you can cover your management mistakes. Assume that you will make plenty of them. We do – even though we are experienced managers. We do not like any business that deals with commodity items, as they usually have a thin margin for competitive reasons.
- **Low operating expenses**, **particularly low inventory requirements:** Most small business failures result from an initial underestimation of operating expenses and undercapitalization. We do not care for retail stores and businesses that have to finance large inventories or account receivables.
- **Large market potential:** You do not want to own a dead-end business, and you do not want to stay small forever. You want a business that can scale up easily, have the ability to serve a nation-wide customer base and leverage the power of the Internet. You do not want to waste your time with businesses like dry cleaning or ice cream shops, which cater to local residents and offer very limited growth potential.

- **Controllable risk business:** You do not want to start a business that has a high failure rate, such as a restaurant. Although all new businesses carry risks, you should only accept the calculated risks that you can tolerate. You need to be able to reduce and control the risks with your efforts. Most people consider risk to be a relative concept and are willing to take higher level of risks if the investment amount is small. So it is important to find a business that requires a low capital investment without sacrificing its potential.

The six criteria above are essentials and are non-negotiable. We do not recommend that anyone engage in a business opportunity that does not meet all of these criteria. We also recommend seven additional desirable characteristics before committing yourself:

- **Recession-proof business:** Many small businesses that thrive in boom times go under when the economy sours. A small business simply does not have the resources to survive a prolonged downturn. Unlike some economists' claims, the business cycle is not dead. We want a business that thrives both in boom times and in the lean years.
- **Clean, quiet, and environmentally-friendly operation:** This is particularly important if you plan to operate a home-based business, as more customers demand businesses to be eco-friendly. Any business that uses toxic materials will have difficulty with operations. Moreover, you will not easily be able to sell the business when the time comes.
- **Something you enjoy doing:** For many people, this is one of the least negotiable of all essential conditions. You should find a business you will enjoy every day.
- **Compatible with a normal life schedule:** A nine-to-five business with weekends and holidays off would certainly be ideal, and many businesses meet this criterion. It provides you with a normal life. Unless you are a masochist, why would you want to own a business for which you are required to get up at 4:00 in the morning (bakery), work until 10:00 at night (restaurant), toil on weekends (grocery) or a combination of all of these?

- **A business that is not a fad:** Too many new and seemingly promising businesses are hot this year, gone next. You want a business that meet people's needs year in, year out. Make sure your products or services are going to be in demand for many years to come.
- **No or little liability:** We stay away from businesses involving danger (i.e. extreme sports) or high liability (i.e. medical products or services).
- **No or low competition:** All things being equal, less competition is preferable. No or low competition, however, may simply be a reflection of a limited market potential. Competition is not necessarily bad, as it fosters efficiency and drives the market to expand. We are never afraid of competition.

The above list of thirteen items is very generic and is based on sound business practices and experience. However, you may not care for some of these criteria, and there may be some issues you consider important that are not addressed here. Using this list as a starting point, make your own list of important criteria before you begin the hunt for that "ideal business." Once you complete your list, do not compromise. It's important that you persevere until you find a business that meets all of your criteria.

DR. CHASE'S "TEN-BAGGER RULE"

In the previous section, we listed a low capital investment with a high potential as the No. 1 criterion. However, if a small initial investment limits your business potential —a typical situation — your new venture is not very meaningful. It is important to identify an opportunity that requires a relatively small investment, yet provides significant upside potential. Dr. Chase's "Ten-Bagger Rule" addresses this issue.

Chase Roh, one of the authors, has started three businesses in the last thirty years, always applying this rule to each new venture. It is particularly pertinent to our evaluation of small business opportunities.

The rule is that *the business must have the potential to generate sales of at least ten times the original investment per year within two to three years.* In addition, *the business must generate at least 20 percent pre-tax net profit on its sales.*

When Chase was raising venture capital for his first company, this rule played well with the investors. Later, when he invested his money in new startups as an angel investor, he again relied on this approach. More importantly, he has always abided by this rule in the management of his own companies. If you do not enjoy taking large risks, you should seriously consider this rule.

For example, if you are investing $30,000 in your new venture, Dr. Chase's Ten-Bagger Rule says that your business must have the potential to generate at least $300,000 in sales per year. In addition, it should generate pre-tax net profits of at least 20% of your sales. The profits should be at least 40% of sales, when you include the compensation for your own labor, until your sales reach close to a million dollars. It is a fairly stiff requirement, but we would not have it any other way. There will be inevitably many management mistakes and you will also encounter unplanned negative events. We want the Ten-Bagger Rule to cover them all. So if your sales figures amount to only five times the investment and the profit rate falls short, you will still be ahead – or at least you won't lose your shirt.

"Ten-bagger" is an investment term coined by the famed mutual fund manager Peter Lynch.[6] It refers to a stock investment that pays off ten times the original amount. Mr. Lynch said he developed a passion for making ten times his money early in his investing career. Despite his legendary performance, he could not do it often. His occasional ten-baggers would lift the performance of his portfolio, even when most of his stocks were lackluster.

Chase is an experienced investor, but he has had only one ten-bagger stock in his life — and that happened by accident. He generally doesn't look for ten-bagger stocks since the odds of finding one are slim. On the other hand, all three of his companies are ten-plus-baggers. His first two companies were of course well over ten-baggers by the time he sold them. His latest company is on its way passing the ten-bagger mark.

There is a lesson to be learned here. Finding a ten-bagger stock is not easy. A stock may have all the earmarks of a ten-bagger before you buy it, but you have no control over the value actually materializing; indeed it is very much a matter of luck. On the other hand, when you start a business of your own, you are in control. First you have to make sure your business has the characteristics of a ten-bagger before you start it. Then it will depend on how hard and how smart you work.

The Ten-Bagger Rule is closely related to a very high "sales to fixed-assets ratio" —which we will discuss in Chapter Two. Since the initial fixed-asset investment requirement is a significant hurdle for many new startups, finding a business that does not require huge investment in plants and equipment is important. But our rule applies not only to fixed assets investment, but to *all* investment requirements. The Ten-Bagger Rule is really about finding a business that you can open on a modest budget, yet with a large upside potential. This will stack the cards in your favor. It removes the hurdle of having to raise large capital, reduces your risks, and promises higher return on your investment. Oddly enough, we found that very few small business starters or their advisors have a firm grasp on this concept.

If you take nothing else away from this book, please take this: **Large potential with low investment**. In the next chapter, we will see if digital apparel printing business meets this golden rule.

CHAPTER 2

New Opportunities in the T-shirt Revolution

THE advent of digital garment printing technology in recent years has reshaped an important U.S. industry. Such changes present an opportunity to those who are already in the garment decoration industry as well as to entrepreneurs who are interested in it. In this chapter, we will examine the opportunities presented by direct-to-garment digital printing technology. We will compare it to the traditional screen printing method of garment decoration. We will also discuss if digital apparel printing business meets the criteria presented in the previous chapter for those seeking a new business opportunity.

NEW TECHNOLOGY, NEW OPPORTUNITY

How do you find new business opportunities or improve an existing business in a significant way? Such opportunities arise daily as changes occur in the marketplace. Generally, the best new opportunities are created when technological advances occur or when the method of doing business changes. New technology usually brings new methods that make the industry more efficient—meaning less expensive—and can produce higher-quality products and services. Such changes allow a business to fundamentally shift its efficiency or cost structure. It also allows entrepreneurs to enter a previously unavailable industry and compete on equal footing with those who have been entrenched for years.

Perceptive industry veterans will benefit the most if they recognize and adopt the benefits of the new technology and methods. An early adapter will provide higher-quality goods and services at a lower cost, gaining a larger share of the market. Unfortunately, there will always be those who are slow to recognize such new methods or flat-out resist them. These shortsighted individuals will be displaced by competitors who quickly embrace the new technology or by new competitors entering the industry using the new technology. Indeed, this is an example of elementary socio-economic evolution. This book is about taking advantage of such an opportunity in the huge garment decoration industry.

The "digital revolution" has affected daily life for more than three decades. The authors of this book proudly brought it to the sign and screen-printing industries by introducing the first computerized graphic design software programs and computer-controlled vinyl and stencil cutting plotters in the mid-1980s. Our IBM PC-based sign and graphic design program called ANA Design Station was the first of its kind. To put this development in perspective, the first Apple II computer was introduced in the late1970s while the first IBM PC did not debut until 1983. The ANA Design Station was developed in 1985. Until that time, sign makers used the pen and sketchpad approach. Fonts and logo designs were projected on a wall, often aided by a projector, and they would trace the text and graphics. Then they would paint them by hand with a brush.

The introduction of a digital method transformed the process. Now users could enter text and create graphics on an inexpensive PC. A computer-controlled cutting plotter then cuts out the graphics and text on thin, colored sheets of vinyl made by companies like 3M. Once ready, the cut vinyl can be applied to windows, walls or vehicles. Today, this is the primary method used in commercial sign and stencil making. Few if any sign makers rely on hand painting, unless they want to create a special effect using the old artisan method.

The new technology allowed greater opportunities for entrepreneurs to enter the sign industry, which had been closed to all but those who had gone through six years of journeyman apprenticeships. Using the new technology, one could now train a new sign maker in just days or weeks. Countless new sign, graphics and advertising specialty stores were created in the last twenty years thanks to the digital revolution. The authors are aware of many accomplished sign makers who resisted adapting to the new technology; sadly, they have lost business or even closed their doors.

THE REVOLUTION IN T-SHIRT PRINTING

Nearly 20 years after we first brought the digital revolution to the sign and screen-printing industry, the authors of this book spotted a similar opportunity in apparel decoration. Traditionally, apparel decoration was done by two methods: screen-printing (also known as silk-screening) or embroidery. Commercial embroidery machines underwent a digital revolution more than 25 years ago. Embroidery designs are now either digitized or designed digitally. Computer software controls the embroidery machine so that it faithfully replicates the digitally designed stitches. Many advanced digital systems are available today for commercial embroidery.

However, equivalent digital systems had not been developed for the screen printing industry. The basic screen printing method, developed hundreds of years ago, essentially has not changed on pace with technological evolution. The initial process involves creating artwork either manually or digitally. Next, the silk screen is prepared from the artwork using a photo-mechanical process involving high intensity light, or by a digital process. The actual printing process is done either by manually applying screen printing ink with a squeegee, or with automatic mechanical arms. This is a messy and labor-intensive process, to say the least. The screen printing method widely used today for garment printing is an "analog" system as opposed to digital garment printing.

The ink or screen printing paste used for garment printing, or plastisol, is also problematic. Plastisol is liquefied PVC or polyvinyl chloride —by far the most environmentally damaging plastic. The PVC life cycle results in the release of toxic, chlorine-based chemicals which end up as by-products such as carcinogenic and highly toxic dioxin and PCB. The plasticizers, or phthalates, used in plastisol ink to make the PVC flexible, are also carcinogenic. They are released into the environment during the printing and curing of the ink and they will continue to exhaust toxins when exposed to a radiant heat source, such as a dryer or even sunlight. Efforts to develop environmentally friendly water-based ink have not been very successful, as such inks do not have good wash resistance. Lastly, the inks must be cleaned off the screen and the printer manually after each job. This unpleasant and messy process creates wastewater containing PVC. In many metropolitan areas, due to the environmental regulations, it is now increasingly difficult to open a new garment screen printing facility without spending lots of money to install pollution control devices.

Digital apparel printing is nothing short of a revolution in garment decoration, particularly in T-shirt printing. Today digital apparel printing supplements, complements and partially replaces conventional screen-printing. As we will discuss later, when applied to print runs of fewer than 500 pieces of garments, digital apparel printing can replace conventional screen printing, and it's a lot more economical. When digital printers with higher throughput are developed in the coming years, digital direct-to-garment printers are expected to completely replace the toxic process of screen printing. This represents an industry worth close to $22 billion in the US alone.[8,9] The advantages of digital direct printing are many. Below we discuss the comparative advantages from perspectives of process, cost, and impact on health and environment.

Digitally Printed T-shirts with Complex Graphics

Process Comparison

- Screen printing requires preparation of a silk screen for each color to be printed; digital printing requires no such screens.
- A screen printing artwork has to be specially prepared with consideration of chokes and traps, half tones, etc. (specialized knowledge). No special art preparation is needed for digital printing; it is WYSIWYG —what you see is what you get.
- Screen printing requires printing one color at a time. Thus typical garment printing can have one, two or three colors at most. Digital printing uses "process color" or full color, typically has 16 million colors, and is printed on one pass.
- Screen printing cannot handle intricate designs or color photos; digital printing can handle both.
- Screen printing requires spot color ink mix or special orders, while digital printing requires no ink preparation.
- Screen-printed garments have an undesirable hard tactile feel of plastisol; digital prints with water-based ink have a soft feel.
- Both screen printing and digital printing can print on light-colored garments and dark- colored garments.
- For light-colored garments, both methods produce very durable wash-resistant prints. For dark-colored garments, digitally printed garments using today's technology does not last as long as screen printed garments, but their longevity is commercially acceptable.
- After screen printing, the ink has to be cleaned out of the system —a messy and labor intensive process. No such clean-up is needed for digital printing.
- Screen printing requires skilled operator training. Mastering screen printing takes months, if not years. Digital printing is easy to learn.
- Screen printing cannot handle variable content printing. The digital process allows for different text in each copy.
- Due to screen preparation and special ink mix, screen printing requires typically a one- week turn-around time. Digital printing can produce finished products within minutes.
- Screen printing equipment is relatively large, messy, and uses toxic inks —making it unsuitable for a residential setting or for a

home-based business. Digital printers are compact, quiet and environmentally friendly, ideal for home-based or commercial use.

Cost Comparison

- Due to the costs of film and screen preparation and clean-up operations, screen printing requires substantial setup costs per job. Digital printing has virtually no setup cost.
- Due to setup costs, screen printing is not suitable for short run jobs of less than 100 pieces, while digital printing can handle micro runs, short runs and production runs.
- For production runs of more than 500 pieces of simple graphics of one or two colors, screen printing may have a cost advantage. But overall, digital printing is the more economic production method.
- Digital direct-to-garment printers are price-comparable to low-volume garment screen printing machines with two stations. There is no cost advantage for traditional screen printing equipment.
- On a per garment basis, screen printing inks are priced lower than digital printing inks. But the ink cost advantage is more than offset by the costs of screen making, clean-up, longer production lead time and higher labor costs.

Health and Environmental Impact Comparison

- Garment screen printing is done mostly with plastisol, which has a number of health and environmental issues. Digital printing inks are typically water-based and environmentally friendly.
- A number of worker health issues exist with screen printing, but not with digital garment printing.
- The waste-water from the clean-up after screen printing contains PVC and pthalates, and cause significant environmental problems.

The only scenario in which screen printing outperforms digital apparel printing in cost is for large production runs of single or two-color simple graphics. But most custom garment decoration jobs are smaller runs. The sweet spot for digital direct-to-garment printing consists of run sizes between 25 and 250 pieces, or up to 500 pieces.

SUMMARY COMPARISON OF DIGITAL PRINTING AND SCREEN PRINTING OF GARMENTS

	Direct-to-Garment Printing	Screen Printing on Garments
Printing Technology	Inkjet direct printing on garments.	Conventional screen printing.
Technology History	New digital technology.	Traditional, hundreds of years old.
Printing Process	All colors printed at the same time; process color.	Colors must be printed one at a time.
Colors	Up to 15 million full colors; no color separation needed.	Usually one or a few spot colors; color separation needed.
Artwork Preparation	Digital and simple; WYSIWYG, or what you see is what you get.	Analog or digital; requires special artwork preparation.
Screen Making	Unnecessary; No cost	A separate screen must be made for each color; expensive.
Inks	Environmentally friendly water based ink, no health hazard.	Environmentally damaging plastisol ink, health hazard.
Clean up	No cleanup needed.	Messy cleanup between colors and jobs.
Economics for Short Run	Cost effective production of short run, micro run or even single pieces.	Screen preparation and setup costs make short run cost much higher; micro runs are prohibitive.
Economics for Large Run	Can compete with screen printing for multicolor or complex graphics printing	More cost-effective for large runs of one or two color simple graphics printing.

Fixed Asset Investment Requirements

The investment in fixed assets needed to achieve a certain level of sales is an important benchmark for an industry or business. A high "sales to fixed-assets ratio" indicates that assets are efficiently utilized to generate sales, or that the superior technology deployed in the business allows a low level of fixed assets to generate a given level of sales. A low ratio is generally an undesirable characteristic that ties up too much capital compared to the sales volume. Dr. Chase's Ten-Bagger Rule focuses on a highly efficient business and technology whose "sales to fixed-assets ratio" is extraordinarily high.

According to a survey of Specialty Graphic Imaging Association (SGIA), the industry median "sales to fixed-assets ratio" ranged from 2.4 to 1.7 in the 2004 to 2008 period.[10] A large component of the specialty graphics industry is garment screen printing. Compared to these statistics, the digital method of garment printing is far more desirable. A setup with one direct-to-garment printer system, costing about $20,000, has a production capacity of up to several hundred thousand dollars per year. That means the potential "sales to fixed-assets ratio" for digital garment printing is 10 or more. It is four to five times more efficient than conventional screen printing in terms of necessary fixed asset requirements.

Next, let's briefly look at the production economics of digital garment printing. We'll use a basic white T-shirt printing as an example. A blank T-shirt will sell for $1.25 wholesale. It takes about $.50 of digital ink to print a typical graphic on the shirt, which takes about a minute. Allowing for a labor cost of $.75, a finished printed shirt will have a direct manufacturing cost of about $2.50 to $3.00. The selling price of finished goods depends much on the business model. Obviously sales mainly to end user or retail customers will command higher prices than sales to trades or wholesale, while wholesale will have higher volume.

With no large fixed capital investment, no great economies of scale and no large mandatory overhead costs, new small businesses set up for digital apparel printing can compete effectively with much larger established screen printers. We expect that more and more garment printing will be done in smaller job sizes as digital printing becomes more widely available. The greatest beneficiary of all will be the typical established garment screen printers, who already have steady customer bases. Many garment screen printers today turn down orders of less than 50 or 100. Such small jobs are not worth their time and efforts, with the art and screen preparation and cleanup work. When they add a digital printer, they will no longer need to turn down the small jobs. These will become lucrative incremental business. Moreover, some screen printers have successfully used the flexibility and quick turn-around of digital printers to print proofs, prototypes, pilot runs, and to help clients develop new products.

As of 2007, digital apparel printing accounts for less than 1% of the garment decoration industry in the United States. This low percentage presents a tremendous opportunity for both screen printers and entrepreneurs. We do not know how many printers are sold to entrepreneurs who start garment-printing businesses based on this new technology. But we know that up to 25% of the customers buying digital apparel printers from AnaJet were starting new businesses.

Mass Customization of Apparel

Today, few apparel items are made in the U.S. and Western Europe. Most apparel manufacturing has shifted to lower-wage countries. Many of these garments are decorated with personalized images or custom designs. The digital revolution, which allows "mass customization" to take place in many industries, is finally catching on with garment decoration. With it you can print short runs of 25 shirts for a corporate sales team, or a one-of-a-kind photo shirt for a loved one. On-demand production of customized and personalized apparel is a dominant new fashion trend that will keep growing.

As you will see in subsequent chapters, many screen printers and entrepreneurs are seizing the opportunity. But an even bigger change is taking place in personalized garment decoration, which prints one or just a few custom shirts per order. Such personalized shirts may be printed in a store or even in a kiosk environment, such as Lit'l Desi9s —featured as one of our success stories in Chapter Four. The technology and trend has not escaped the attention of sophisticated investors, as you will see in the following examples.

The Story of Zazzle

Among the best-known online personalized shirt printers are www.zazzle.com and www.cafepress.com. Founded just a few years ago by brothers Jeff and Bobby Beaver while students at Stanford University, Zazzle sells personalized T-shirts and other items online. Their father, Robert, serves as the CEO. But this is no longer a small-time family affair. Zazzle caught the eye of big-time venture capitalists; in 2005 a consortium of venture capital (VC) firms headed by Kleiner Perkins backed Zazzle to the tune of $16 million. Kleiner Perkins is no ordinary VC firm; it is one of the savviest investors in Silicon Valley. Its head, John Doerr, is revered in the VC community as a master of spotting new trends and opportunities. Kleiner Perkins invested in countless home run companies like Google, AOL, Amazon, Genentech and Intuit.

In just two years, Zazzle grew to employ 250 people, and as many as 500 during holidays. As of early 2008, Zazzle's Web site had recorded 2 million visitors monthly who buy more than a million items per month; and this number is growing rapidly.[7] According to Zazzle, the company has sold more than 30 million items in the last several years. You can buy personalized T-shirts sporting your own designs or photos. You can also upload designs that can be purchased by other customers. Zazzle has since created an alliance with MySpace, and has arranged licensing deals with Fox, Lucasfilm, Disney and thousands of bands. Visitors can use any of the licensed images in their customized shirts or other items, like mouse pads. Such customization of mass-appeal images and designs is creating an entire new market.

CafePress.com is older and larger, with an average visitor count of 4.5 million per month. It uses a business model similar to that of Zazzle, but is more interested in providing a marketplace for members to sell their shirts. When a visitor buys a member's shirt, CafePress will print the shirt on demand at its digital apparel printing centers in the West and Midwest. Neither CafePress nor Zazzle would exist without digital apparel printing technology.

DIGITAL APPAREL PRINTING AS A NEW BUSINESS OPPORTUNITY

Now, let's examine how digital apparel printing meets the criteria established in Chapter One. It easily meets all six of the non-negotiable criteria:

- **Dr. Chase's Ten-Bagger Rule:** The typical minimum cost of entry into this business is between $20,000 and $30,000. If the proper equipment is selected for the business model, the production capacity can be several hundred thousand dollars per year. If you can develop the ability to sell and utilize the production capacity, it can meet the Ten-Bagger Rule. The key to success is that you be a motivated entrepreneur, and able to develop the business. The nature of the business allows you to concentrate on local businesses, yet you can also serve a nationwide client base in the promotional wear industry we will discuss later, and use Internet marketing to leverage you.

- **Easy-to-operate business:** Most, but not all, digital apparel printers are simple and easy to operate. Most require very little physical space. The business model can be kept relatively simple if you wish.

- **Profit margin:** The gross profit margin will depend much on your business model and local market condition. You have a choice of selling mostly to consumers and end-user businesses at a higher margin, or to trades and wholesale customers at a higher volume.

- **Low operating expenses and low inventory requirements:** In later chapters, you will learn that you can keep operating expenses relatively low. A well-developed blank garment supply chain makes it possible to operate with little or no inventory.

- **Large market potential:** According to the authoritative 2007 Decorated Apparel Universe Study, the apparel decoration industry is a $44 billion market in the U.S., of which an estimated $22 billion is printed garments. A good portion of the garment printing is subject to digital printing.

- **Controllable risk business:** The business has low investment requirements, low overhead, low operating costs and no inventory. These all point to low and controllable risks.

Now, let's look at the seven additional desirable characteristics we discussed.

- **Recession-proof business:** "The decorated apparel industry is resilient enough to withstand whatever Mother Nature or the economy dishes out," concludes the 2007 industry study. Apparel is a basic staple, and there is always a market for printed shirts.
- **Clean, quiet and environmentally friendly operation:** Digital apparel printing is environmentally friendly, as we discussed earlier. It is clean and quiet, which is great for an at-home or small business.
- **Something you enjoy doing:** It's not golfing, but everyone we talked to seemed to enjoy digital apparel printing. If you like arts and crafts, or just enjoy being creative and helping others, you may well love this.
- **Compatible with a normal life schedule:** This is a nine-to-five, five-day-a-week business. It can easily be run as a part-time or seasonal business.
- **It's a business, not a fad:** As long as people wear clothes, decorated garments will be in demand. Nothing is more basic than clothing.
- **Little or no liability**: You can design your business to limit your liability to the value of the garments printed. There is little possibility of product liability.
- **Low or no competition**: There may be competition in your area since it is difficult to avoid competition completely. However, digital apparel printing is still in its infancy, and there are relatively few competitors in most communities. The competition of course will increase as more people adopt this new technology.

As we will see in other chapters, increasing unit sales is the key to success in the digital apparel printing business. Prospective operators should be keenly aware that the entire business depends primarily on one's ability to generate sales using a variety of methods that we will discuss in later chapters. If one can leverage the opportunity by using a Web site, reseller programs or alliances with large outlets, the potential can be limitless. Clearly, digital apparel printing has all the earmarks of one of the best opportunities around.

CHAPTER 3

The
Garment Decoration
Industry

THERE is some homework for us to do before getting into digital apparel printing.

1. The market size and trends of the garment decoration industry: We will discuss it in this chapter.
2. What it will take to get a good piece of the garment printing business: Chapters 11 through 14 deal with sales and marketing, but we discuss it throughout the book.
3. What other successful operators are doing that we can emulate: We present some case studies in Chapter Four.

First, let us review the total market for the garment decoration industry. According to the comprehensive 2007 Decorated Apparel Universe Study by *Impressions* magazine, the industry is comprised of 55,657 businesses. They generated a total revenue of $43.9 billion in the United States during 2006.[8] This revenue is at the garment decorator level, thus it is the wholesale value. The industry grew 6.1% in 2005, and 5.4% in 2006 – a much higher rate of growth than that of the U.S. economy. By any measure, this is a huge market with healthy growth.

Decorated Apparel Industry Overview 2004 – 2006

Year	Industry Revenue ($ million)	% Change from Prior Year	Number of Businesses (thousands)	% Change from Prior Year
2004	$39,201		55.0	
2005	$41,608	6.1 %	55.3	.6 %
2006	$43,858	5.4 %	55.7	.7 %

Source: 2007 Decorated Apparel Universe Study

The survey also reveals that this industry is financially robust. More than 70% of the shops demonstrated sales growth of more than 5% compared to the previous year, and 28% reported sales growth of more than 21%. Furthermore, 97% of the shops reported profits. These are impressive numbers. We do not know of any other industry where 97% of the businesses involved report profitability.

Yet not all of the decorated garment market lends itself to digital apparel printing. The 2007 study divided the decorated apparel industry into three groups based on their primary business models: Screen Printing shops, Embroidery shops and Promotional Product Distributors. Many screen printers also operated embroidery machines, while some embroiderers also had screen printing operations. Many promotional wear distributors outsource garment decoration to screen printers and embroiderers.

2006 Sales by Apparel Decorator Type

Type of Apparel Decorating Business	Sales (US $ mil)	Share of the industry
Textile Screen Printing	15,166	34%
Embroidery/Monogram	8,765	20%
Promotional Products Distributor	13,134	30%
Inkjet Garment Printing	370	1%
Others (includes outsourced items)	6,423	15%
Total	43,858	100%

Source: 2007 Decorated Apparel Industry Universe Study

A closer look at the industry reveals that screen-printing shops accounts for 34% of the $44-billion apparel decoration industry, or about $15.2 billion. Embroidery shops take 20% of that gross, or $8.7 billion. Businesses that operate primarily as promotional product distributors are mixed bags: some decorate garments in-house (about 40%), while others outsource decoration to screen printers and embroiderers. By further deconstructing the three types of garment decorators and those considered "others," we estimate that the total printed garments account for over $22 billion in the U.S.[9] The rest would be embroidery, monograph or heat-applied garment decorations, such as laser printer or dye sublimation.

More than a year ago, we compiled a composite picture of the decorated apparel industry's output values and projections from various sources.[9] The chart below shows the decorated garment output values and future growth by revenue type. Promotional wear revenue is expected to top $16 billion by 2010, outpacing the screen printing and embroidery industries and sustaining its past growth rate. Screen printing will continue to show a steady and respectable growth rate, but it appears that embroidery's golden age has passed. The embroidery industry has gone through a good growth phase worldwide for many years until recently, but it is now near the saturation point in the U.S.; now only modest expansion is expected. The trend in favor of printed garments over embroidered garments is also evident in the changing blank garment output, where printable garment production has grown faster than that of garments more suitable for embroidery.

The growth pattern, however, shows that the real star of the industry in coming years is direct-to-garment printing. This sector's value is expected to grow from less than $200 million in year 2005 to close to $6 billion by 2010. By that time, about a quarter of all printed garments will be direct-to-garment printed in the U.S. The analysis also shows that heat transfer and heat-applied graphics production rates will stay flat through 2010, with some segments of it declining.

Decorated Apparel Industry Growth by Revenue Channels (in Billion $)

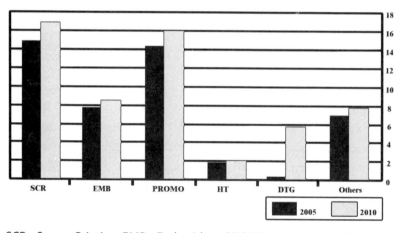

SCR= Screen Printing; EMB= Embroidery; PROMO= Promotional Products; HT= Heat Transfer; DTG= Direct to Garment Inkjet

Source: PPAI, ASI, IMPRESSIONS, EMB

Printed garments account for more than half of decorated garments, and most are still screen-printed. Direct-to-garment inkjet printing accounted for less than 1%, because it is still a new technology that has yet to penetrate most garment decoration production plants. A market research firm, I.T. Strategies, is projecting the world-wide revenue of textile materials printed by direct-to-garment digital printers to grow to $12.8 billion by 2010. If it materializes, the share of direct-to-garment printing will increase from less than 1% in 2006 to about 10% by 2010. As we have discussed, there are a number of advantages to digital printing. It is simply a matter of time and availability of a wider range of products before digital apparel printers achieve a higher rate of adoption. Meanwhile, digital apparel printing is establishing itself as the preferred method for short run decoration, particularly for promotional apparel.

Although most garment printing is done by screen-printing for now, the screen printers are busy adopting direct-to-garment printing. According to the SGIA 2008 survey, garment decorators planned to spend half of their digital output device purchasing budget on direct-to-garment printers, compared to all other types of digital output devices.[10] The survey shows that other types of digital methods, such as inkjet transfer, dye sublimation and laser transfer, are in decline. These older "heat applied graphics' require expensive materials and are labor-intensive, resulting in higher operating costs.

The adoption of direct-to-garment printers will accelerate as higher throughput printers are introduced. I.T. Strategies predicts that the direct-to-garment printer world-wide installed base will increase to over 50,000 printers by year 2010 from a moderate beginning just a few years ago.[11] We are yet to see if this will materialize, but we have no doubt a significant part of garment decoration will shift from screen printing to direct-to-garment digital printing in the coming years. A similar development took place in the wide-format inkjet graphics printing market. The installed base of wide-format inkjet printers replacing screen printing grew from under 3,000 units in 1994 to over 60,000 units in just five years, a twenty-fold increase. We believe a similar development is in the offing for direct-to-garment printers.

Since garment decoration is a relatively simple business that does not require a large physical space or many employees, nearly a quarter of all garment decoration businesses are run part-time. Besides, approximately 36% of all full-time owners run their businesses from home. As their businesses grow, an increasing number of owners are progressing from part-time to full-time while home-based businesses are shifting to commercial or industrial space.

The 2007 industry survey shows that a typical full-time screen printing garment decorator had an average of $1.3 million revenue in 2006, compared to an average of $470,000 for a full-time embroidery business.[8] This may indicate that embroidery shops are generally smaller businesses than screen printers — or it may indicate a changing trend in favor of screen printed garments over embroidered garments. Since less than 1% of all garment decoration utilizes digital inkjet printers at present, there are still too few of them from which we can derive comparable statistics for digital garment printers. At present, we do not have any statistics that apply to part-timers.

While the above division of the decorated garment industry is based on the production methods, we would like to consider a different perspective. We will classify the decorated garment market into three groups based on perceived customer needs. We have not yet seen anyone classify the market in this manner, but it will serve a useful purpose as you plan your marketing strategy.

Mass-Produced Decorated Garments

This segment includes T-shirts imprinted with the kind of Las Vegas, Hawaii or Orlando themes one finds in souvenir or gift shops. In general, these have uninspiring designs that are made and sold cheaply. At the next level are the T-shirts that sport the logos of various athletic teams, sporting goods or footwear companies, or shirts that feature the likenesses of famous entertainers, celebrities or public figures. Many of these are licensed products. Some even sport especially appealing—and copyrighted—designs or logos. These shirts may be sold at big box retailers or upscale department stores like Bloomingdale's. The common thread is that all of these shirts are mass-produced and mass-marketed. Such shirts are printed in volume through screen-printing, which is often outsourced. These shirts are definitely not for today's direct-to-garment digital printers, and it's best for you to simply ignore them.

Spirit Wear and Fun Wear

This custom-decorated apparel type is intended to identify members of particular groups or to enhance team spirit. Often, such shirts are produced more for fun than for any defined objectives. Such shirts invariably have logos, custom designs or special messages. Custom-printed shirts may be made for softball teams, to identify a corporate marketing team at a trade show, members of traveling groups, 10K race participants, family reunions, etc. Or they may bear the photo of a loved one. Such shirts are very important for direct-to-garment printers. They are typically ordered in quantities of 5 to 100, rarely exceeding 250. Screen printers usually refuse shirt orders fewer than 50 shirts.

Due to the set up and clean-up costs, it is not economical for screen printers to print smaller orders. Additionally, customers usually do not want to pay more money just because they ordered less than 50 shirts. Furthermore, these shirts often have multiple colors, complex designs or photos that cannot be easily reproduced through screen-printing. This market thus represents fertile ground for digital apparel printers.

Promotional Wear

This is an ideal market for digital apparel printers. Typical promotional gift items from businesses include T-shirts with company logos, pens, mouse pads, bags and calendars. According to the Advertising Specialty Institute (ASI), the U.S. promotional gift industry had revenues of $19.4 billion in 2007. What's more, the industry has a compounded annual growth rate of 4.7% over the last five years.[12]

Most promotional apparel orders are not large. The typical order size is in the range of 25 to 250, which is an ideal run size for direct-to-garment printers. A good half of these promo-wear orders are less than 50 shirts —a quantity that screen printers are likely to decline or for which they will charge premium. Unlike screen printers, digital apparel printing can produce brilliant full-color images, a favorite among corporate marketers. Another advantage of digital printing is its quick turnaround time. This type of garment decoration is tailor-made for digital printing. We devoted Chapter 13, Navigating the Promotional Apparel Industry Successfully, to promotional product printing.

In summary, we find digital printing for garment decoration to be a large and growing industry. Both established garment decorating screen printers and aspiring entrepreneurs should consider this emerging technology. Direct-to-garment printing is most suitable for custom graphics in what we categorize as fun wear and spirit wear, and promotional wear. Although the "sweet spot" for run size is currently below 250 to 500 pieces, this will change as higher throughput printers are introduced. The digital printer can handle short runs, and it can serve a number of other purposes that screen printing systems simply cannot provide. Due to the digital nature, the client base can expand beyond the local market.

CHAPTER 4

How Others Have Found Success

O NE of the best ways to learn about a business before you launch your own is by finding out how others have done it. These case studies are inspiring and will give you some essential information. We also wanted to chronicle cases that were not successful but could not find suitable examples, although there certainly would be some.

Of the five cases we present here, two are stores built around direct-to-garment printers, two are home-based businesses, and one has just moved from home-based to a commercial space. They are owned and managed by men and women of varying age groups and from all walks of life. They are located in big cities, suburbs and small rural towns. The common traits among these business owners are intelligence, curiosity, a thirst for newer and better things, and no fear of facing new challenges. Although none except one can be classified as tech-savvy, they all seem to appreciate the potential that new digital technology brings to this age-old industry.

Here are their stories.

ACCU PRINTING AND DESIGN INC.

WWW.ACCUPRINTING.CA

Ashley, a man in his early forties, worked as a power engineer in Canada's oil drilling industry for almost twenty years. "I have enjoyed oil patch work and it can be quite lucrative, but oil fields have just too many ups and downs," said Ashley. He sold one of his rental properties to finance the opening of his first business—a company that offered copying and printing services to the local business community. One of the key decisions he made early on was to offer a "one-stop shop" for promotional printing services. After reviewing the needs of his customers and doing some market research, he decided to specialize in promotional printing. When he learned that apparel is the most important among all promotional products, he purchased a digital apparel printer.

Accu Printing and Design Store Front

After the installation of an AnaJet printer, his first job was to print 1,800 T-shirts for a sporting event. The shirts required imprints on the front and back, which raised the unit price he could charge. With other smaller jobs, he printed more than 2,200 shirts during that first month. Immediately following the first job, the customer placed more orders, and Ashley realized that his business potential was greater than he originally envisioned. During the first two months, he printed more than 4,500 shirts; he soon decided to add an embroidery service that would satisfy many customer requests. Indeed, other customers requested both printing and embroidery on the same shirt. For this, he bought a Melco two-head Amaya embroidery system, which works well alongside the AnaJet printer.

By this time, he was confident that his business would prosper. "In this small town, there are not an awful lot of businesses you can do at the level of investment I am comfortable with," Ashley noted. "I certainly did not want to open another pizza parlor. I wanted to do something other businesses did not offer—and something that contributed to the local business community."

Ashley has relied primarily on local customers in Ponoka, Alberta, which has a population of 7,000. He estimates there are about 50,000 people in his trading area. Although there is a large-enough population base to support his business growth, he is now eyeing remote customers. "There is no reason to limit yourself to local businesses. With a digital garment decoration plant, you can really serve the entire nation," he said. For now, most of Ashley's customers are local businesses, sporting teams and their sponsors, schools and individuals. He advertises in a local newspaper and on a radio station. His three-month contract with the radio station costs $800 and is the most expensive component of his marketing.

Ashley employs a graphic designer three days a week. His wife helps as needed. His sales manager, who works four days a week, generates enough business to keep his shop humming most of the time. A Web developer is now busy building his Web site. When the site is ready, Ashley plans to launch a marketing program to sign up additional customers in northern Alberta and other parts of Canada. He is also gearing up to provide apparel decoration services to other promotional product distributors who do not have in-house capabilities. He is not concerned about the predicted recession. "When times are hard, businesses must advertise and promote their products and services. I am really in the advertising and promotion business, not in the printing business," says Ashley. He is outgrowing his current 3,700-square-foot facility and is looking for a larger space to accommodate more employees.

CARLSON GRAPHIX

WWW.CARLSONGRAPHIX.COM

Living in a suburb of Sacramento, California—the state capital—Michelle worked for the State of California for many years as a Web designer. Although she had no prior art training, she mastered Adobe suite graphics programs through tutorials for her job. Still, she always wanted to own a business. It was an easy decision to open a graphics intensive advertising specialty printing shop in her home. She did some garment screen-printing, pad printing and vinyl graphics using a vinyl cutting plotter.

Her natural knack for business and wide circle of friends helped grow the business. As screen printing of garments emerged as her main business, she became concerned about its many limitations, such as its limited number of colors, the requirement for special artwork preparation and its slow turn-around time. She wanted to offer her clients what she referred to as a "more dynamic graphics" capability. Also, since she is environmentally conscious, she was concerned about the plastisol inks, cleanup and wastewater associated with screen printing.

Soon she learned that the direct-to-garment printing technology would address all of these issues. After some research, Michelle purchased an AnaJet Digital Apparel Printer. She, her husband Jerry and their teenage son all took the training course. It was a good decision. Michelle's business grew very quickly, and she needed the help of her family to run the new printer. She can now print true, full colors as well as the photography that many of her customers wanted.

She also spent some time to develop a simple Web site, www.carlson-graphix.com. To date she has not purchased any advertisements, nor has she done any Internet marketing. However, she has plenty of customers. The best break came right after she installed the digital printer. The unsolicited email we received from Michelle says it all:

> *The day we left the factory training with our machine, we received a call that we had been awarded a job printing 200 black shirts for.... the California Department of Transportation (Caltrans) for an event honoring Caltrans workers who had lost their lives while making our*

highways and bridges safer. The artwork was far too complex for the screen-printing process, so we did the job using our AnaJet Apparel Printer. As the ..... event approached, we got jittery, hoping that Caltrans would like the shirts and that our "care" tags were adequate. This was, after all, our very first job using our AnaJet. Our company name was mentioned on all major news media as sponsors (great plug!) and was also included in the official printed program. There was only one problem. The shirts were so popular, that the staff who were supposed to receive shirts for the event couldn't get through the line of people who wanted their own shirts! Our shirts were TOO popular! We could not have had such success without this wonderful technology and your top-notch training and support throughout the process. We have already received four calls in the first day since the event. Attendees are requesting their own shirts & designs for other special events, as well as for fundraisers, schools and teams.

Michelle Carlson, Carlson Graphix

The news coverage and publicity Michelle received continues to generate a lot of business. She also gets many new customers through positive word-of-mouth. Many local screen printers who do not want to do short runs or multi-screen jobs refer customers to her. According to Michelle, her business has tripled in the months since she received her AnaJet printer. Since many more customers wanted to visit her "store" to look at the samples than her "home business" permit would allow, she needed more space. Recently, she moved into a commercial space at a "printing complex" which also includes a commercial printer and a sign maker. There, Carlson Graphix is now attracting many drop-in customers. Her reputation has been spreading. As this book goes to print, Michelle informs us that she has received an order of 1,150 event shirts from Bermuda Music Festival. She intends to do the entire production on AnaJet printer.

Her screen printing machine and other equipment remain on the sidelines for now. Michelle and Jerry have discussed him officially joining her business someday, once it is built on a much larger scale around many direct-to-garment printers. Meanwhile, Jerry helps when he has time as the "Master of Color" at Carlson Graphix. She feels lucky to have the full support of her family.

LIT'L DESI9S

WWW.LITLDESI9S.COM

As an art director, Debby worked on advertising campaigns for luxury brands such as Jaguar, Lexus and De Beers. She took time off several years ago to raise her children, as her husband was a successful general contractor and real estate investor. She had no plans to get into business on her own.

However, one day Debby was teaching her five-year-old son, Aidan, how to spell. She was playing with his name on a computer screen. Using a graphics program, she flipped each of the letters in his name to look like a dinosaur. Further experiments allowed her to convert just about any name into various animal shapes. Aidan loved it, and so did his friends—and their mothers. A new business idea was born: graphic designs on clothes that would teach kids to spell while entertaining them.

Debby acquired a small manual silkscreen machine with two stations to allow one- or two- color printing. With the help of husband Gal, she began to print kids' and babies' shirts with various designs. The shirts were an instant success in her town, which is located about an hour from Boston. Local papers wrote stories about them, and the children's shirts became a hit. Town fairs, school programs, fund-raising events and holiday fairs proved to be excellent markets. When Debby had to recruit Gal to take over production, they realized they had something big on their hands.

However, as her business grew, Debby became concerned about the effects of plastisol screen printing ink on the health of Aidan and her other tiny customers. She experimented with water-based screen printing inks, but the wash-fastness was not satisfactory. Gal's research led them to direct-to-garment inkjet printing. It would solve both their production and inventory problems. They could now print on demand. Debby could now also use a full-color palette.

Lit'l Desi9s Kiosk

A Baby's Onesie with Name

They decided on an AnaJet Digital Apparel Printer, since it offered every feature they could ask for. It was a "green" system because of its water-based inks, it was compact and it provided the color vibrancy Debby had long sought. About this time, Debby also launched her Web site, www. LitlDesi9s.com. After that, the business truly took off. Soon, they decided to go to a mall to receive better exposure. Debby signed up for a kiosk in the Prudential Center in downtown Boston, across from Saks Fifth Avenue. The mall attracts a great deal of traffic from locals and tourists alike. The kiosk was a small cart, about 4 x 8 feet, and it was just big enough to hold the printer, a heat press and a small inventory of her garments.

Debby currently has over 1,500 names in various animal designs and is adding new ones every week. Recently, she broadened her product line beyond basic shirts and introduced organic clothing.

Between Debby and Gal, who eventually joined Lit'l Desi9s full-time, their Prudential Center kiosk is open seven days a week. Her wholesale operation signed up some retail stores that now market her clothing line as far away as California and New Mexico. Web site reorders by her kiosk customers are gradually increasing, and thus far, she has received orders from over 30 countries. Their first licensed store is set to open in the summer of 2008 at an upstate New York location, and more are planned.

BONITA PROMOTIONAL PRODUCTS

WWW.BONITAPP.COM

Bill is a proud 28-year Navy veteran who worked in the aircraft electronics and avionics maintenance field. After leaving active duty, he continued to work for the Navy as a Technical Representative, teaching electronics maintenance to a new generation of sailors.

With his Navy pension and the income from his wife's granite business, they settled into a very comfortable suburban life in San Diego area. But Bill quickly learned that playing golf three times a week was not fulfilling. At a home and garden show, Bill and his wife met some people from a promotional product printing organization. Bill committed himself to learning about the promotional product industry with the same zeal he had for electronics. He discovered that it was a steadily growing industry that showed good potential. Soon he set up shop at his house and began to offer various promotional products to the greater San Diego business community. As Bill acquired low-tech equipment such as a pad printer and a button-making machine from the promotional product organization who introduced him to the industry, he wondered if he was wasting his talent as an electronics wizard. But he liked the business and its potential to grow.

For more than two years, he offered pens, pencils, buttons and other items that he imprinted with his equipment. The promotional apparel orders, the most profitable segment of his business, were sent out for screen printing or embroidery. From the beginning, he ruled out bringing a messy screen-printing machine into his neat suburban home. He was also unhappy about the limited color range and cumbersome process of screen printing. Because of his technical background, he was already aware of the technology for the digital printing of clothing. Soon, such machines began to appear on the market—but he was not satisfied with their capabilities. He decided to wait until he found the right printer.

Meanwhile, he joined the PPAI, a national trade organization for promotional product distributors and suppliers. It allowed him to network with others, and opened up new opportunities. Since he was tech-savvy, he designed and created a Web site for Bonita Promotional Products, with which he could offer a wider variety of products. And at last, he found a garment printer that appealed to him.

Bill says his installation of the AnaJet Digital Apparel Printer in a spare room was the most exciting thing he'd done since he entered the industry. A year prior, about half of his business was garment decoration and the other half an assortment of other imprinted items. In the last year, Bill's business has more than doubled thanks to clothing item sales. Today, more than 90 percent of his business is in promotional apparel, most of which he prints with his direct-to-garment printer. He still subcontracts orders for embroidered garments. He stopped using the pad-printing machine because it was too much trouble and the profit margins were too small. The inks dried too quickly and the machine required too much maintenance. Hundreds of dollars of pad printing inks will dry and spoil if they are not used within a few months of purchase. Most of his non-garment items are now business cards and buttons, which he contracts out.

For marketing, Bill likes to network with other PPAI members around the country, and he hopes to work with other promotional product distributors who do not print their garments in-house. Locally, he sends out promotional brochures by direct mail. Some of his best leads come from local fictitious name announcements, networking and word-of-mouth. After he began to work with other promotional product distributors, his garment printing margin declined to about 50 percent because he has to give discounts to these trade orders. That's okay, Bill says, because the trade orders from other distributors are repeated frequently. Bill attributes his success to two key decisions: joining the PPAI and purchasing a direct-to-garment printer. He thinks he will have enough business to move into a commercial space this year, but he is in no particular hurry. He is too busy enjoying life.

UBU DESIGNS

WWW.UBUDESIGNS.COM

A graduate of the University of Utah, Hayley is a well-educated, upper-middle-class suburban housewife and mother. After fourteen years as a college counselor at USC, she left her position to enjoy a more flexible schedule with her family, living in a California beach community. As manager of her daughter's softball team, she took on the job of designing and ordering T-shirts for the team members and parents from local screen printers.

The experience stimulated her interest in potentially making it a business. She discovered the direct-to-garment printer at a trade show and recalled, "I just fell in love with the technology." Since it was compact, clean and easy to operate, she knew she could run the system at home. She figured she would be able to get orders for more T-shirts for the other softball teams in the league since she knew many of the parents. After extensive research, she decided to purchase an AnaJet Apparel Printer and go into business with a graphic designer and fellow softball parent.

A great deal of her T-shirt business came through word-of-mouth—the kids' softball league, soccer league, school PTAs, local businesses and community organizations. Most of her orders are small runs. But the smaller orders are fine with her since she loves customer interaction and expressing her creativity. Her smaller orders are also offset by her ability to charge higher retail prices.

Haley placed her first paid advertisement recently in a kite surfing magazine.

Husband Dan is an avid kite surfer and encouraged her to explore kite surfing T-shirts. As that part of the business has grown, her husband has become increasingly involved. He helps design the T-shirts and recently marketed them at a Pismo Beach Kite Surfing Festival. The couple has signed up with retail outlets in Maui and Florida, and they are emphasizing kite surfing in their decorated apparel business. This represents a niche market, but they would rather be the big fish in a small pond. They are currently looking for additional worldwide outlets and licensing of their kite surfing design.

Hayley is also very active with Internet marketing. She has five Web sites. UBUDesigns.com is her main site, which includes an e-commerce store. The majority of her kite surfing shirt sales comes from KiteTs.com. Her new site, UBUsurfDesigns.com, appeals to the regular surfer crowd. She also has FastPitch.com, which sells T-shirts and accessories to the softball community. Her WidowTs.com site pokes fun at her husband's growing addiction to kite surfing, and it hopes to appeal to golf widows, baseball widows and others. It is evident that all of her sites and marketing themes are oriented to her personal interests, which is a very powerful marketing method. An important dividend from this approach is that Hayley enjoys what she does since she can personally relate to her customer community.

Looking back, Hayley recalls there were some hurdles during the startup phase. But after a few months, when the local community became familiar with her business, it began to pick up speed. By the end of the first year of operation, she had earned enough money to buy out her partner. Since then, she has been reinvesting her profits into expanding and building the business. While she sometimes considers moving the business out of her house to a commercial space, she enjoys the flexibility and convenience of working from home.

CHAPTER 5

Store Operation

IF YOU ALREADY HAVE A STORE OPERATION…

Adding a digital apparel printer can yield significant new opportunities for your existing business. Unlike screen printing, a digital apparel printing operation does not require much space. The printer and a heat press require only a 6 x 6-foot area. There is no need to carry an inventory of unprinted shirts, since all your blanks will be purchased after an order is received. Therefore, the additional space requirement is negligible. Concerning personnel, if you or someone in the store has some knowledge of graphics software such as Photoshop or CorelDraw, this will certainly be helpful. If not, the basics can be learned in a few days. For existing stores, there usually is no need to add new employees at first, although a new full or part-timer will be needed as the business grows.

- **Screen Printing Shops**
  For screen printing shops that print garments, a digital apparel printer can allow you to offer short or micro- run orders, which you likely turn down at this point. For medium size jobs of up to 500 pieces, the direct-to-garment may prove to be more effective, particularly if the job calls for multi color printing. For large-run jobs, the printer can also be used to print proofs prior to screen setup and pilot runs. Many progressive screen printers are also offering

their direct-to-garment printing facility to their customers to help develop new products. The designers can see their new designs in the form of finished products in a matter of minutes. The digital printer will also allow you to offer continuous tone, multicolor and complex, detailed graphics, which screen printing machines cannot handle. The printer's ability to print color photos will also add a new dimension. Operation of the printer itself requires very little additional space. You will be pleased with the convenience of not having to prepare film and screens for each job, and there is no messy cleanup. Some screen printers, particularly those who specialize in promotional wear or whose orders are typically short runs of less than 500 shirts, have switched completely to digital apparel printers.

- **Embroidery Shops**
  For embroidery shops, the digital apparel printing allows you to offer an alternate method of garment decoration. Embroiders have reported that an increasing number of customers request printed garments. Many embroiderers have learned that screen printing is an involved and messy process, incompatible with their existing business. Moreover, a very large percentage of embroiderers are home-based businesses, and it is difficult to install a screen-printing system at a residence.

  Now both home- and store-based embroiderers find digital printing a very appealing method, similar to their existing business. The software and production process are very similar to embroidery. Another advantage relates to the fact that mixed media decoration is becoming very popular. Mixed media includes printing graphics or photos on garments, and then embroidering highlights into the printed shirts. More about mixed media decoration will be discussed in Chapter Seven.

- **Sign Shops**
  If you are a typical sign shop, you most likely will have many requests for custom T-shirt printing since imprinted shirts are a form of advertising. At present, you probably farm out these

orders. You may have a small screen printing machine, but your setup is solid surface printing and will not be conducive to garment printing. Adding a digital apparel printer will allow you to offer additional services. If you have a vinyl cutter or digital printer, you already know the software and possess most of the tools and knowledge necessary for a successful digital apparel printing operation.

- **Digital Printing Shops**
  Technically, digital printing shops are closest to direct-to-garment printing. If you offer large- and small- format digital printing, you already have an operational base similar to that of a digital apparel printing operation; you know much about the printer maintenance, care procedures and software. The addition of digital printing on garments and other textile materials represents a natural growth for your shop. Discover what other types of substrates you can print on with your garment printer in later chapters.

- **Printers and Quick Printing Shops**
  The advent of the Internet and electronic publishing has reduced the volume of business printing over the last ten years, and many printing shops are in need of new avenues to replace the lost business. Since garment printing is simply another form of printing, it is quite natural for quick printers to offer a shirt printing service. Most people think of quick printers when they need some imprinting done on garments. Most commercial printers already have a sales force in place, and have been particularly successful in offering a garment printing service to their existing school and corporate accounts.

- **Photography Shops**
  Many one-hour photo shops, mini-labs, camera shops, portrait studios and event photographers have successfully offered photo T-shirts in recent years. They either farm these out or use the dye sublimation method. Direct-to-garment printing compares well with dye sublimation in terms of cost, quality and the types of fabric which it can print on. Simple and inexpensive digital apparel

printers now allow photo professionals to offer photo shirt printing directly to their customers. As will be discussed in Chapter Ten, the reception of digital apparel printing among photo industry professionals has been enthusiastic. It can indeed replace some of the photo finishing revenues lost due to digital photography.

- **Gift Shops**
  Gift shops are ideal for custom photo T-shirt printing. They already benefit from heavy customer foot traffic. Gift shops in tourist districts will do particularly well when they offer custom photo T-shirt printing or other personalized shirt printing.

- **Apparel Shops and T-shirt Stores**
  Most T-shirt stores offer semi-customized shirts by using heat-applied graphics such as transfers or the dye sublimation method. These methods are inflexible, require expensive materials and are labor-intensive. In addition, dye sublimation works best with 100% polyester material; it cannot be applied to 100% cotton. The quality suffers when applied to poly-cotton blends. Direct-to-garment printers will also drive down the operational costs for T-shirt stores. Apparel shops can do well by offering the custom printing of designs for finer clothing. More ideas will be discussed later in the book.

IF YOU ARE OPENING A NEW BUSINESS...

Many digital apparel printer purchasers are starting new businesses, and many of them are first-time business owners. It is easy to see why: the low level of investment, a relatively easy operation to learn, and enormous market potential attract entrepreneurs to this business. This truly represents the elements that meet all of the criteria applicable to small business owners, as we discussed in Chapter One.

We have been asked frequently if new business owners should seek busy, high-traffic store locations—which, of course, are accompanied by high rent and other expenses. The answer depends on the vision for the business and other factors. The highest traffic location with the highest rent will be regional mall kiosks, which are explored in the next section. The opposite end of the spectrum is a home-based business, discussed more extensively in the next chapter. If you do decide to operate a store, then you are a typical operator and this section is for you.

First, you will need to decide between: 1) a retail space that carries higher rent, higher foot traffic and visibility, and 2) an industrial or commercial space with minimum foot traffic but lower rent. If you are in a tourist district or highly urban area and your business model relies on walk-in traffic, the answer is obviously a retail location. However, if you are in a high-rent district or if your business will be based on active marketing to business customers, you will be better off with the industrial space.

If you rely on the various marketing and sales strategies discussed later in this book, you will likely deal with other businesses rather than walk-in traffic. If you are spending a considerable amount of time promoting to other businesses, the store location becomes less important. Chances are most of your customers will never visit you. Your business will be done over the phone—supplemented by pictures, illustrations and price lists on your Web site. Interestingly, the 2007 Impressions Study indicated that 60% of full-time screen printing garment decorators were located in commercial or industrial space, while 23% of them were located in retail space. Home-based businesses accounted for 16%. Since digital apparel printers require much less space and have cleaner operations than screen printers, we expect that more digital apparel printing shops will be located in homes and retail environments.

If your store is located on a back street visited by very few customers, then your sales and display area can be small. The space should be dedicated to the most efficient production operation. If you expect frequent customer visits in a retail location, however, it is important to show your products and samples in the most appealing way. Do not hang samples on wire clothes hangers. Acquire plastic torso mannequins for males, females and children, and clothe them with your printed sample garments. Show your entire range of products, such as plain white T-shirts, colored T-shirts, various polo shirts, golf shirts, jeans, and aprons. You can purchase inexpensive plastic torso-form mannequins at prices ranging from $25 to $100 from stores such as those listed below. You may not need a full-form mannequin. Half-round display form mannequins with concave backs are intended to show the front of the torso and are much less expensive. They can be purchased for as little as $90 per dozen.

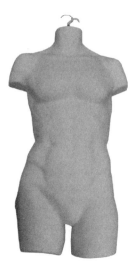

Display Form

www.onlymannequins.com
www.slstoredisplays.com
www.studiorox.com
www.gershelbros.com

If you are counting on walk-in traffic, the window displays are very important. Inside the store, you should have a dozen or more mannequins or half-round display forms wearing your sample garments. You are likely to sell more of the types of shirts displayed on your mannequins. So display some upscale products along with basic styles. Show design samples in a sample photo book or on a computer screen, which should also be connected to large, flat panel television monitors. If you have an instant photo T-shirt printing facility, the camera images should also be shown on the TV monitors.

Below is an example of a store layout for an approximately 700-square-foot store. This is probably the minimum space you'll need for a good selection of shirts. Throughout the store, you will need display cases and shirt inventory shelves. Your supplies can be hidden below your working table and counters.

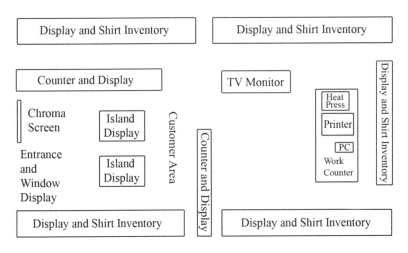

Approximately 24' x 30' Store Layout

You should also have some poly T-shirt bags in a dispensing rack for the shirts you will sell to your retail customers. You can buy the bags and racks through packaging or commercial supply companies. Some of these vendors will imprint your store name for a nominal charge. By all means, do it! It represents a source of free advertising for you when the customers flash those bags on the way home. Here are some store fixture and supply vendors.

www.storefixturesupercenter.com
www.gershelbros.com
www.uline.com
www.universalplastic.com/t-shirts-bags.htm

A KIOSK OPERATION

Kiosks are the highest-octane form of retail spaces. To be effective, these must be located in high-traffic areas such as regional shopping malls, airports, tourist districts and other hubs such as New York's Grand Central Station. You can also use your kiosk as a light production facility. Kiosks often inspire impulse buying, so the kiosk decoration, visual merchandising and good selection of garments are important. Kiosks can also charge a bit more than a retail store. Attractive display racks capable of showing all the items you can produce are essential. A photo shirt printing capability will be invaluable in addition to custom shirt printing. If you have the right location and marketing program, the potential can be exciting. The primary downside, however, is that the rent and operational costs are high. For high-rent and high-expense operations, it is essential that you develop a very detailed business plan.

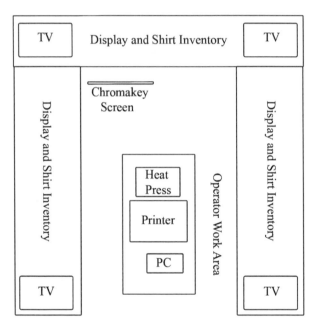

Approximately 12′ x 12′ Kiosk Layout

CHAPTER 6

A Home-Based Business

A 2004 report by the SBA Office of Advocacy states that home-based businesses make up roughly half of all businesses in the United States.[13] The same study indicates that home-based businesses are the predominant form of small businesses. Two-thirds of all sole proprietorships, partnerships and S-corporations are home-based.

If this does not demonstrate that home-based businesses deserve respect, what will? We do not discourage anyone from setting up 10 digital apparel printers and opening a large printing plant to serve a nationwide customer base. However, if you are considering entering the garment decoration business, and you are not experienced in small business management, please do not discount the merits of starting as a home-based business.

Garment decoration and T-shirt printing can be a worthy home-based business. You can design a business in which you do not have customers visiting you. You can set up so that your orders are taken by a sales person, or arrive by telephone, Internet, e-mail, fax and mail, and your finished products get shipped or delivered to customers by couriers. All you need is a small office and production facility of a few hundred square feet at your home. In fact, a spare room may be enough. In many communities, you will probably be able to conduct business from your home as long as you do not have many walk-in customers, do not use dangerous substances, are acceptably quiet and do not interfere with the character of the neighborhood. But make sure you comply with appropriate city ordinances and the CC&R of your homeowners' association.

If you are replacing a small screen-printer in your home, you will appreciate that a digital apparel printer requires no storage of screen printing ink with its noxious fumes. You'll experience no more of the difficulty associated with the toxicity of screen printing ink and wastewater. Choose a digital printer that uses a cartridge-based ink system, which can be easily disposed of after use. Most cities have collection facilities for the used cartridges. Moreover, AnaJet is planning to offer a cartridge recycling program as a part of their green system. The program includes a postage paid return envelope with each new cartridge. This will allow you to simply drop the used cartridge in the envelope and hand it to the mailman.

When managing a home-based business, there are some unique issues to consider.

GIVING CREDIBILITY TO YOUR
HOME-BASED BUSINESS

Some people are concerned about whether their home-based businesses lack the credibility necessary to attract serious customers. We do not believe this is true —as long as you separate the business from your home life. To mitigate some of the stigma attached to a home-based business, consider the following.

Address

Avoid using a Post Office Box or private mail box address. Many people are apprehensive about sending money to businesses that operate through PO Boxes. The worst you can do is to use a private mail box, and disguise it with a suite number. You can use a much more business-like address despite the fact that your business is located within your home. Consider using your home address in a form such as:

ABC Promo Wear Company
123 Washington St.
Unit A
Omaha, NE 68101

If you live in an apartment or rented house, using a PO Box is not necessarily a bad idea. You can do any number of things through your Web site to give the permanence to your address and provide credibility. Just make sure the customers can always find you when you move.

Telephone

You should use a telephone number that is dedicated solely to the business, rather than using the house or mobile number. Subscribe to the number under your business name, otherwise certain vendors and service providers will not recognize your business. When you cannot attend the phone, use a dedicated and reliable answering machine or service. Ensure you answer all your telephone calls by clearly stating your business name; your answering machine should do the same. We do not recommend the use of a cell phone as your primary business phone line.

Business Web site

When you have a small or home-based business, nothing gives you more credibility than having a professional, businesslike Web site. Don't include pictures of your kids or vacation photos —unless you're building a company around the theme of being family-owned and operated. Don't try to build a Web site yourself unless you have Web development expertise. At the same time, you do not need to spend a fortune on a nice, credible Web site. In Chapter 14, we will show you how.

You can do many other things to add credibility to your home-based business. In Chapter 12, Marketing, you'll learn about many approaches and techniques for increasing your credibility and formal business tone. Custom apparel printing does not always require that people physically come to your shop. The apparel can be identified effectively through good photographs and descriptions in your catalog or on your Web site. Additionally, customers can send their graphic images to you over the Internet or via email. All you need to do is print the shirts and deliver them.

CHAPTER 7

Printing Basic T-shirts and Mixed Media Decoration

I n this chapter, we will discuss the basics of the printing process. Garment decoration by screen printing is an involved operation. The screen printing art must be specially prepared for traps, chokes, half tones and color separation. Then the screens must be prepared with emulsion and exposed with a film and light source. Spot color inks need to be mixed or specially ordered.

Of course, none of this is necessary with digital apparel printing. It is a completely WYSIWYG process: "What You See Is What You Get." If a customer provides a usable, good-quality graphic, all you need to do is to load it into your PC and click the PRINT button. If the customer-provided graphic is of poor quality or you need to design a graphic specifically, the graphic art preparation is much simpler than that for screen printing; there's no choke and no color separation. Below, we will review the printer, post treatment, and the RIP software. Then we will overview the mixed media garment decoration. We will conclude the chapter by discussing other production-related issues.

BASICS OF DIGITAL APPAREL PRINTING

The principle of direct-to-garment printing is very similar to using a desktop printer. You load the graphic or text into your PC and then you send the job to the printer. Most printers will print the image on a T-shirt or other garment within one to two minutes by jetting inks onto white or light-colored garments. After that, you heat cure the textile ink onto the garment fabric with a heat press or textile oven. Voilà! You have the finished product. Note that some of the printers which cannot control ink flow rates may need to overprint two or three times if the fabric is thick. In this case, printing time will naturally increase.

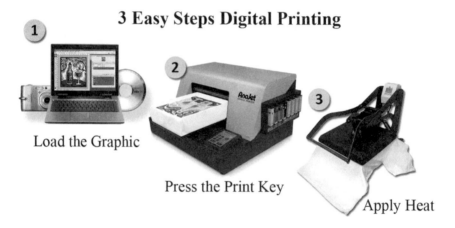

3 Easy Steps Digital Printing

1 — Load the Graphic

2 — Press the Print Key

3 — Apply Heat

Basic Process of Direct-to-Garment Printing

If you are printing on black or dark-colored garments, you must pre-treat them. For white, pastel or light-colored garments, pretreatment is unnecessary and is not recommended. Pre-treating dark garments is done simply by spraying pre-treatment liquid onto the area to be printed. The printer begins by printing white ink on the image area. Then it retracts the garment table or platen to the home position, after which it prints CMYK – cyan, magenta, yellow and black – colored inks on top of the white ink.

Since typical Titanium Dioxide (TO2)-based white ink gels very quickly after printing when it is exposed to air, there is usually no problem printing colored inks on top of them. In the case of the Kornit machine, it prints colored ink on top of the still-wet white ink, but the process appears to work fine. Because dark garments need at least a double pass—once with white ink and then with the colored inks—the printing requires double or triple the time it takes to print white garments. You can watch the printer demonstration videos in the manufacturers' Web sites listed below.

PRINTER SELECTION

In digital apparel printing business, one of the most critical decisions you will make is the selection of a printer. Because you are likely to have only one printer when you start your business, your production will be interrupted if that printer breaks down or has clogged print head nozzles. Understand that direct-to-garment printing is still an evolving technology; some of the printers marketed as direct-to-garment printers do not work properly. Most problems relate to ink flow, system maintenance and customer service quality.

As with any other young industry, some firms sell such products without having the proper technology or adequate customer support capabilities. Before committing to a specific brand of printer, you should develop a good business model, since doing so will give you an idea of how your printer will be used. Evaluate the printers against your planned business needs, and then spend some time evaluating both the printer's performance and the manufacturer's reputation.

Most people concentrate on print quality when shopping for a direct-to-garment printer. However, this is misguided, since just about all direct-to-garment printers will yield excellent quality images. You should concentrate on two specific elements. First and foremost, determine whether it has **good ink flow**. Many printers are fundamentally flawed, with considerable problems that stem from ink flow issues and clogged print head nozzles. The second consideration is the **manufacturer's ability to provide support**. Call the maker's tech support line to learn whether you can get a live technician without a significant wait. Ask some questions to determine if the support personnel are knowledgeable and helpful. Check out the company's reputation by visiting relevant Internet forum sites.

In our opinion, there are three direct-to-garment printers worth considering in today's world market. All three printers are state-of-the-art and probably will meet your needs.

Kornit Digital

Kornit Digital is an Israeli company dedicated to the manufacturing of direct-to-garment printers and inks. They offer two models, and both are very large, heavy and impressive. The smaller of the two models, the 932DS, is a single-table printer. It uses piezoelectric drop-on-demand inkjet print heads. The manufacturer offers CMYK and white, five colors of pigmented solvent ink, and water-based inks. The unit can print both on light and dark garments. The maximum resolution is 630 dpi, which is adequate. The operator can control ink flow volume to suit the type of fabric being printed. Kornit also offers a dual-table printer, which prints two pieces of garment simultaneously. However, Kornit printers have had reliability issues, and the startup process to get the ink flow through the print heads can be long laborious, according to some users. But operators have also reported that once the system is fired up, it is a good workhorse.

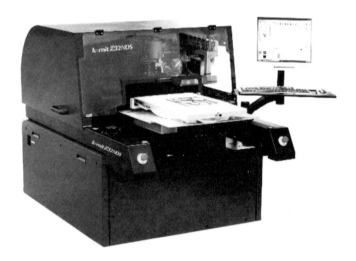

Kornit Printer Model 923DS

An advantage of Kornit is its built-in inline pretreatment station for dark garments. A significant disadvantage is the high cost of the printer and its replacement print heads. In the United States, Kornit has three dealers who will install the system and train customers on-site. The printer is quite an involved piece of machinery, and you will most likely need a dedicated, trained specialist to tend the machine. A backup operator should also be thoroughly trained; this printer cannot be operated intuitively by someone with a half-hour of training. All three U.S. dealers have good reputations for customer support. In some countries, Kornit will dispatch engineers from Israel for installation and training. Visit their Web site at www.kornit-digital. com.

Brother GT-541

The Brother garment printer is offered by the industrial embroidery machine division of the large Japanese company Brother International. It is a direct inkjet garment printer capable of printing one shirt at a time. Water-based pigmented inks of CMYK colors are offered. The machine uses four on-demand piezoelectric print heads, each with 128 nozzles. Print resolution is 600 x 600 dpi. It can print only white or light- colored garments. The Brother unit is a reliable printer if the maintenance procedure is followed properly. Since it does not offer white ink for dark shirt printing, it will have less possibility of ink flow problems. The operator can control ink flow volume to suit the type of fabric being printed. The print quality is good, and the software seems easy to use.

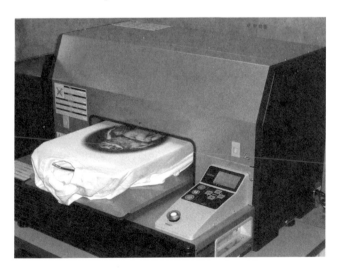

Brother Garment Printer

Obviously, a critical drawback of the Brother printer is its inability to print on black or dark-colored garments. Its replacement print heads are quite expensive, as are its inks. Although it is not as expensive as Kornit, it is significantly more expensive than other printers. In the U.S., most Brother embroidery machine dealers can handle sales and support. These dealers will install the printer and train the operators on-site. The operational procedure is relatively simple, and you can probably train backup or replacement operators without much difficulty. See www.brother-usa.com/garmentprinters for further details.

AnaJet Apparel Printer

This model is offered by AnaJet, which is dedicated solely to the development and manufacture of digital apparel printers and software. The printers are engineered and manufactured in southern California. AnaJet printers use piezoelectric drop-on-demand inkjet print heads. CMYK and white water-based pigmented inks are offered. Recently they also introduced a specialty ink for printing on 100% high performance polyester, nylon and other synthetic fibers, which water-based direct-to-garment textile inks cannot print. The machine prints on light- and dark-colored garments at a resolution of 720 dpi. The operator can control ink flow volume to suit the type of fabric being printed.

Since the AnaJet white ink is also titanium dioxide (TO2)-based, an extra precaution has been designed into the ink delivery system. AnaJet considers that the ink flow problems associated with TO2-based white ink stems largely from the TO2's exposure to air. AnaJet's "closed loop ink delivery system" is designed to prevent this. The white ink is packaged in sealed bulk ink cartridges and is not exposed to open air until the ink is jetted out. Like other printers, the AnaJet requires regular, light maintenance to maintain an optimum ink flow. The machine uses 8 channel multiplexed print heads with 180 nozzles per channel for 1,440 total nozzles; the combination helps to achieve excellent print speed. The software is intuitive and easy to use. The key to the excellent color quality lies in their print software.

It is the most compact of the three printers. Its small footprint and portability can be an advantage. Its operation is quite straightforward and simple. Since the company's strategy calls for acquisition of a large customer base, both the printers and print heads are priced very reasonably. In our opinion, the AnaJet printers offer the best value in the industry. For fairness, we should disclose again that the authors are officers of AnaJet.

The company uses a network of distributors, dealers, partners and OEM customers to market and service their printers. In most countries, the distributors will install and train the customers on-site. In the U.S., however, AnaJet encourages all new customers to attend a free operator training class at its factory training facility. In addition, it offers extensive DVD video training programs for operation and maintenance. It also holds regular webinar to train and retrain customers and distributor personnel. Once trained, the customer can self-install the printer and train co-workers. You can find more information at www.anajet.com.

AnaJet Digital Apparel Printer FP-125

The inks from all three printer manufacturers have good color gamut, and are high-quality. Consequently, they all provide excellent quality prints and have good color reproduction capabilities. They can print detailed graphics in vibrant colors which cannot be reproduced by a screen-printing process. Prints on light shirts have excellent wash-fastness, and they last as long as screen-printed shirts. The wash-fastness of dark shirt prints, however, has room for improvement. If pretreatment is done properly, the dark shirts' wash-fastness is commercially quite acceptable. At present, AnaJet and other industry leaders are striving to produce a faster and more effective pretreatment process.

For any particular graphic, one of the above three models may print faster than the others. However, the overall printing speed and production throughput of the three machines are comparable. A typical 10 x 12-inch graphic can be printed in as little as one minute on light-colored shirts. The AnaJet and Kornit equipment can print dark-colored shirts in approximately two to three minutes. In an actually shop operation, such printing speed would yield an average production throughput of about 25 light shirts or 16 dark shirts per hour.

Why are the above three machines are preferable?

The primary reason we recommend the above three printers is due to their ability to control the ink flow rate and good ink flow which are essential for textile printing. For a textile printer to function properly, the operator must be able to control the ink flow rate depending on the type of fabric being printed. For thin woven fabric, very little ink should be jetted, using small ink drop sizes. For heavy materials such as those used in sweatshirts and hoodies, the ink volume should be increased considerably with larger ink drop sizes. You will have a good idea about the importance of ink volume control by reviewing the accompanying charts. They show how AnaJet and Brother determine and control the optimum ink volume based on the garments being printed. The printer's ability to control ink drop size is also key to good ink flow, since the printer can more easily clear clogged ink nozzles using larger ink drops.

AnaJet Bulk Ink Cartridge System

Ink Volume Control

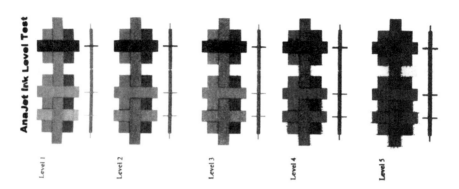

AnaJet Printer allows operator control of the average ink drop size and ink volume to suit textile material. At five ink levels for three ink drop sizes, it has 15 effective ink volume settings.

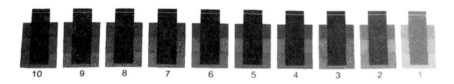

Brother Printer allows the ink volume selection through the ink volume test pattern shown above.

Although inkjet technology has been used for a variety of purposes, no application demands a higher ink flow rate than textile and garment printing. When the printer demands a high rate of ink flow, the printer's ink delivery system must be able to respond quickly to prevent "print head ink starvation." We believe the above three printers have been properly engineered to prevent such "starvation." All of these printers benefit from innovative engineering to prevent nozzle clogging—the chief problem in the industry at present, particularly with TO2- based white ink. When the nozzles clog, they must be reopened through a head cleaning and other operations, which takes time and wastes ink. Assess the three printers against your business model and expected usage before making your choice.

All three of these printers have distribution channels in most industrialized countries of the world. They all provide adequate service and support in North America and most European countries. In other parts of the world, you should conduct thorough research to determine how well such service logistics have been developed.

Other Brands of Direct-to-Garment Printers

Beyond the above three machines, there are other equipment marketed as direct-to-garment printers. These are often made in the Far East, but some are made in the U.S. or Europe. The common element is that all of them are Epson document or photo printers modified to accommodate garment-loading mechanisms so that ink can be jetted onto a T-shirt passing underneath the printer. The ink systems have also been changed. Since garment printing demands much more ink than printing on paper, the small, original Epson ink cartridges are inadequate for the task. As a result, most of these adapted models utilize a bulk ink delivery system that often connects the printer with open bottles of ink via tubes. Some printers with bulk ink cartridges are modified to allow replenishment of the ink through access holes. Such modifications can interfere with the integrity of the original ink supply system designed by Epson unless provisions are made for proper ink delivery. We've heard stories about how these systems experience difficulty with ink flow and nozzle clogging problems. The problems are even more severe when TO2-based white ink is used.

These types of printers usually do not have the ability to control the ink flow rate, and that calls for attention to evaluate the ink delivery system more carefully. Since the ink flow volume for photo and document printers is very low, insufficient rates of ink flow can invite many issues with these units. Often, you must overprint the image to get a sufficient amount of ink on the garment, especially on thicker knitted fabrics. When you cannot control ink drop size or flow rate, it becomes more difficult to reopen clogged print head nozzles. Most of the software supplied with these types of printers is also inadequate.

Some of these printer suppliers do not have adequate technical support or service logistics. For instance, we learned that these suppliers often could not provide service parts once Epson discontinued the particular model that served as the basis for their garment printer. If you are interested in one of these systems, you should conduct thorough research on the printers' performance as well as the maker's reputation for technical support.

A positive aspect of these printers is that they all have excellent print quality thanks to Epson technology. All of these machines that we have seen use water-based pigmented inks—typically, CMYK and TO2-based white ink. Inks offered by most U.S.-based suppliers for such printers are of good quality, and have a good color gamut and wash-fastness. But beware of lower-quality inks from Korea and China.

MODIFIED DOCUMENT PRINTERS

Some modified photo printers offered as garment printers have bulk ink cartridges with access holes for ink replenishment.

Other models have ink bottles on the side of the printer.

HEAT TREATMENT

All textile printing inks require heat treatment after printing, typically 350° F for 35 seconds. If you lower the temperature, you must increase the time. Most operators use a heat press because of its small footprint and lower initial cost. But such presses are more labor-intensive than conveyor-fed oven dryers. A professional-quality heat press will range in cost from $1,200 to $2,000, and there are many manufacturers and models. Get one that uses a digital control for temperature and time to ensure accuracy. Units with a "pop-up" option open the top plate automatically when the appropriate amount of time has elapsed. Unlike earlier models, most of the units manufactured in the U.S. work well. Below are some of the leading heat press manufacturers and a sampling of their most popular models for direct-to-garment printing.

Geo. Knight Heat Press with Pop Up Option

Geo. Knight & Co. www.geoknight.com/
Model DK 16 Clamshell Model, with Pop Up Option

HIX Corporation www.hixcorp.com/
Model HT 400D, with Auto Pop Up Option

Hotronix www.hotronix.com/
16"x16" Hotronix Auto Opening Clam

Textile ovens and conveyor oven dryers save labor, but one drawback is that these units use a significant amount of energy and typically run at 220VAC. They also require a relatively large space. If you have a small shop or work from home, this may not be appropriate. Costs for these machines range from $2,000 to $5,000, depending on features.

Conveyer-fed Oven Dryer by Black Body Corp.

PRETREATMENT OF DARK GARMENTS

For direct inkjet printing on dark garments, the garment must be pretreated prior to printing by applying a pretreatment solution. This is true for the screen-printing process as well. Pretreatment is similar to the acrylic polymer used in mixing screen-printing paste or ink. This is essentially an adhesive that will prepare the surface of the garment to receive the ink. Without such pretreatment, the white ink pigments will seep into the textile fibers, and the printed shirts will not show vibrant colors. The adhesives in the pretreatment not only bond the pretreatment layer with the textile fibers, they also leave a thin layer on the surface of the textile on which the printer can apply inks. Since garment manufacturers do not provide pretreated garments, the process must be done by the printing shops.

Pretreatment is quite a simple, albeit a bit tedious process. The pretreatment solution is often diluted with distilled water and sprayed onto dark garments. Follow the manufacturer's instructions, since all pretreatment solutions are provided by the printer makers. Most often an HVLP-type electric paint sprayer or a manual sprayer is used. The industry is improving the ease of pretreatment and is taking steps to make it unnecessary for garment printers. There have been attempts to pre-treat garments before shipment to printers, to develop easy-to-apply pretreatment solutions and to develop easy-to-apply pretreatment sheets impregnated with pretreatment solution. However, these improvements have been slow.

Pretreatment Station

Attempts to make an automatic pretreatment sprayer and dryer have not been successful, except for Kornit printer's built-in unit. When we planned to develop a fully automated unit, the estimated cost of the pretreatment station was comparable to that of a printer, and we did not feel it was acceptable to the market. The most practical method is to use an electric sprayer inside a pretreatment booth, which helps exhaust the spray mist from the building if used indoors. Such pretreatment booths can be obtained for less than $1,500.

SOFTWARE AND GRAPHICS PROGRAMS

A direct-to-garment printer is always operated by a computer that uses graphic software. Each of the printer manufacturers provides printer drivers and raster image processor (RIP) programs that link the graphics application with the printer. Some makers who use Epson photo printers as the basis for their equipment simply rely on Epson printer drivers. However, these are inadequate for textile printing.

The quality of the printer driver and RIP program is critical for your operational efficiency and printed image quality. Some of the software programs included with these printers may be unstable and difficult to operate. When shopping for a system, you should consider the quality and ease-of-use of the included software as much as the printer itself. Equally important is the software's ability to control ink flow. As has been previously mentioned, if the program lacks the ability to control the ink flow rate, you will experience severe limitations regarding operations and the variety of textile substrates you can print on.

Most printers will run with any Windows-compliant graphics program. The most popular programs used are Photoshop, Photoshop Elements, Adobe Illustrator and CorelDraw. CorelDraw and Illustrator are good, but they are vector-based programs. Some graphic designers do not consider vector-based programs ideal for printing operations since printing operation uses raster images. Raster images are native to Photoshop program.

If you are already familiar with Illustrator or CorelDraw, you can continue to use them for digital apparel printing. However, if you are familiar with Photoshop or are just starting out, the Photoshop family of programs may prove more suitable for garment printing. Photoshop Elements is a junior version of Photoshop without many of the design functions included with the full program, but it is adequate for use with acquired images and simple designs. It will be necessary for you or one of your workers to become familiar with at least one of these graphics programs. You can attend workshops or seminars offered at local community colleges, or you can use tutorial CD-based programs. After just a few days, you will have acquired sufficient knowledge to run the program.

The sources of graphics are varied. Some shops offer stock garment decoration graphics. Some acquire stock graphics and modify them to suit customer needs. Others go extra miles to develop a series of distinctive proprietary graphics in order to offer their own line of apparel, and market them. If you are like most shops, you will print customer-provided graphics. However, some of the customer graphics will be of low quality or low resolution —or even hand-sketched. The printed result may be unsatisfactory through no fault of yours. So you may need to provide an image cleanup or enhancement service. Unless your shop can do it, it may be a good idea to retain some graphic designers. There are also Internet-based service providers. The best of the breed we have seen is Artwork Source. www.ArtworkSource. com provides art design, cleanup, scanning and other graphic services at a very reasonable cost. Its typical turnaround time of 24 hours will allow you to respond quickly to your customers' art needs. Depending on your method of operation, you should be able to charge graphic service fees for art design, cleanup and enhancement.

MIXED MEDIA DECORATION

Garment decorators have begun to mix different types of decoration on a single garment, a process known as mixed media decoration. It can unleash the designer's creativity and command much higher prices since it can potentially deliver higher levels of customization. Mixed media decoration can generate very unique products. Some of the most common mixed media decorations include:

- Direct-to-garment printing and digital embroidery;
- Direct-to-garment printing and rhinestones and/or studs; and
- Direct-to-garment printing and heat transfer films.

Rhinestones, heat transfer films and digital embroidery all combine well with printing. The direct-to-garment printing method is preferred over screen-printing for these techniques, since they often require multicolor printing and production and are usually limited to small quantities of less than a hundred pieces.

Digital Embroidery

Although digital apparel printing is a relatively new technology, embroidery moved to an all-digital process many years ago. The combination of these two methods makes a great deal of sense. Both processes use the same or similar design software, a similar production process, and together they can produce highly desirable and unique results. Here are the steps for incorporating digital embroidery:

1. Design your print and embroidery graphic on the computer, making sure to have registration marks in the print that will be covered by embroidery;
2. Print and heat cure the garment;
3. Hoop the garment and align the registration marks with the embroidery machine; and
4. Embroider to complete the design.

Registration is a special consideration. Different embroidery machines use different methods to register prints. Some, such as the Melco Amaya, have laser alignment tools designed for this purpose, but all embroidery machines will be able to provide an alignment method for printed shirts. One caution to keep in mind, however, is that of distortion. Since fabrics are flexible, the graphics can become distorted after printing or during embroidery. This distortion can cause problems with registration between the printed image and the embroidery. However, appropriate design and capable software can compensate for this difficulty. The combination of print and embroidery is likely the most profitable of any form of mixed media decoration.

Melco Embroidery Systems, a leading embroidery machine manufacturer, began offering a direct-to-garment printer, MelcoJet, in late 2007. MelcoJet was an immediate and blazing success, since many embroidery machine customers wanted to add a printing capability.

Rhinestones

Combing the digital printing with rhinestones consists of three basic steps:

1. Design your shirt;
2. Print your shirt; and
3. Apply the stones.

Although there are several ways to apply rhinestones, the best method for combining them with direct-to-garment printing is known as Hot Fix. These stones come coated with a heat-activated adhesive that adheres the stones to the garment under a heat press.

You can place the stones by hand, purchase customized or pre-designed stone transfers or even create your own transfers. Hand placement is good for a small amount of stones intended to accent a print, but it can be tedious with complex designs. Ordering pre-made transfers is the simplest method—it is just a matter of placing the transfer onto a preprinted garment and pressing it with a heat press. One drawback is that custom transfer tapes can be expensive. The last method available is to prepare your own transfer sheets. This approach represents a balance between material cost and production speed. Here are the steps for making your own transfer sheets:

1. Make your design and print it on paper and on your shirt;
2. Position the rhinestones on top of your printed paper, and place the transfer tape on top of the stones to attach them to the tape;
3. Place the transfer tape and stones on top of the shirt, and heat the stones in a heat press per the manufacturer's recommendations; and
4. Peel away the transfer tape.

Precise registration between the garment and stones can be time-consuming. The more stones you use, the more cost and time required. The best way is to plan ahead, and design the graphic to make the application of stones easy. Design the graphic so that the exact placement of stones does not become critical for the integrity of the design. Rhinestones are worth trying since they require no special equipment for digital apparel printers. They can provide stunning results.

Heat Transfer Films

Heat transfer films or heat-applied tapes are available in a variety of colors, and special effects films may be found to accent your prints as well. These special effects films are of particular interest to direct-to-garment printers because they can yield results that are impossible to achieve through direct-to-garment printing alone. These effects include metallic transfers, glitter transfers and textures such as flocking. Flocking is velvety material that has a raised feel. These special effects, like other forms of decoration, can help increase your sale price. The process requires a cutting plotter to cut the films and, of course, the transfer material. Some suppliers will sell pre-cut lettering and graphics, and others will custom cut the same per order.

Here are the steps for applying heat transfer films:

1. Design your graphics for printing and transfer;
2. Print and heat cure the garment;
3. Cut the transfer films with a cutting plotter;
4. Remove the excess material from the cut transfer films, also known as weeding;
5. Position the transfer on the garment and press it with the heat press; and
6. After cooling, remove the transfer backing paper.

There are several considerations to keep in mind when dealing with transfer films. One is production time. The more complex the design is, the longer it will take to weed. For this reason, most garment decorators avoid complex designs. Transfer materials themselves vary regarding ease of cutting and weeding. It is worthwhile for any digital apparel printers to experiment with cut transfer films. The largest supplier of heat transfer films and flock materials is Specialty Materials. For more information, visit www.specialty-materials.com

SOURCING APPAREL PRODUCTS

You will need to source the blank apparel stocks, mouse pads and other blanks on which you will print. In the Appendix, we list the wholesale sources. This is a well-developed, dynamic and very competitive industry that is constantly changing. You will be able to find convenient sources based on your location, but you should continually monitor for new sources of supply. The types of apparel and other blank products you offer to your customers will depend on your business model. We have given some guidelines under Selection in Chapter 12, Marketing. If you are catering mostly to the promotional wear distributors, many distributors like to source the blanks themselves to keep control of what they offer to their customers. In that case, they usually have the supplier drop ship the blank shirts to the printer.

Relabeling

When you buy blank garments, they come labeled from manufacturers such as Hanes, Gildan and Fruit-of-the-Loom. These are all fine names, but you many want to consider relabeling. That is to remove the original label and replace it with your own. This will essentially launch your own clothing line and greatly enhance your market position among retailers and customers. Relabeling is best done with your own design prints, but it has been used for printing normal custom T-shirts with customer-provided graphic. However, relabeling is not easy to do in-house; it is best to send your garments to a relabeling service. If you live in a major metropolitan area, you will not have much difficulty finding a relabeling house since it is quite frequently practiced in the apparel industry. If you cannot find a local service, have your blank shirt supplier ship directly to a relabeling house. They can recommend reliable relabeling houses. Such services can relabel a hundred shirts within a day or two at a cost of about 15 to 25 cents per piece.

When you relabel, you must follow certain guidelines to ensure that you do not violate the Textile and Wool Acts.[15] You must leave the fiber content, the country of origin and the country of manufacturing origin as they appeared when you received the garments. Even if you are printing or restyling the garment, you cannot change the country of manufacture from the original country listed.

Below, we list some examples of relabeling houses.

Apparel Amendables Inc.
10105 N.W. 88th Avenue
Miami, FL 33178
Phone (305) 888-6900
www.apparelamendables.com

Lucky Relabel
2717 Orange Avenue
Santa Ana, CA 92707-3744
Phone: (714) 546-4194

IMPAC Corp.
587 Industrial Road
Carlstadt, New Jersey 07072
Phone: 201 460-0900
www.impaccorp.com

To relabel, you will need to design and order your own clothing labels. Such labels will cost from 5 to 30 cents a piece based on quantity and quality. Make sure you order "iron-on" labels and not the "sew-on" type to ensure easy application. The label and ink should also be water-resistant.

The following is a short list of clothing label makers, but there are many such suppliers.

Apparel Label International
Phone: 800-646-5775
www.clothinglabels.com

Northwest Tag & Label
2335 SE 11-th
Portland, OR 97214
Phone: 503-234-1054
www.nwtag.com

Clothing Labels 4 U
Phone: 800-469-1301, 407-656-5534
www.clothinglabels4u.com

Online Garment Decoration Design Portal

In recent years, designing custom T-shirts online has become wildly popular. The best-known examples are websites like www.CustomInk.com, www. CafePress.com, and www.Zazzle.com. These web sites use digital printing technologies that allow customers to design their own T-shirts online in small quantities. While the online T-shirt design portals were being worked out, more established companies made moves to facilitate personalization throughout their fulfillment systems; they used production methods that made fulfillment of small-quantity personalized goods possible on a mass scale.

Early in 2008, Melco Embroidery System released LiveDesigner Suite, a complete online design personalization portal for apparel decoration. The Melco LiveDesigner program allows online customers to design their own graphics for direct-to-garment printing as well as embroidery. Besides a variety of garments and apparel, items previously not customizable online — such as bags, jackets and jeans— can now be customized with LiveDesigner. The program generates "production ready" files, designed online by the end user, which can be printed or embroidered. For both direct-to-garment printers and embroiders, online design portal programs like the LiveDesigner program represent another avenue to integrate customer input into a short-run production process.

Production Management Software

Managing order fulfillments can be challenging if you are dealing with large quantities of small orders coming in through an e-commerce portal. Giant companies like Disney and Williams-Sonoma have been known to invest heavily in production management software that helps them to master the complexity of mass personalization. Now commercial programs are available to address mass personalization. For embroidery and direct-to-garment printing, Melco Industries has introduced software called MelcoDirector that allows companies to manage personalization production for both direct-to-garment printing and embroidery. This software connects with its LiveDesigner e-commerce portals, and provides valuable real-time production statistics.

MelcoDirector downloads orders from LiveDesigner portals automatically, delivering the following information directly to the fulfillment center:

- Customer contact information
- Product information
- Print files in .PNG or other selected formats
- Embroidery files – in .OFM and .EXP file format
- Visual work instruction - with images that show the operator exactly where to place the designs

CHAPTER 8

Other Textile Material Printing

I f you are like most other garment printers, basic T-shirt printing will be a large part of your business. The application of a direct-to-garment printer, however, can add many other dimensions. In this chapter, we will discuss these. Don't limit yourself to the ideas that are discussed here. After all, these concepts represent just some of the approaches being offered, and hundreds of other garment printers will be doing these things. Have a brainstorming session with your associates to come up with a unique concept. Indeed, the more distinctive your product is, the more opportunities you will have. If you don't like competition or like to have a good margin, your range of products and applications must be different from those of everyone else.

Here are some ideas you might want to consider.

A. **Printing on other garments.**
   Polo shirts, sweatshirts, hoodies, jeans, aprons, bibs and various baby items are the most in-demand items after common T-shirts. These can easily be integrated into your printing offerings. Corporate marketing departments will typically order polo shirts rather than T-shirts if the items are not intended as mass promotional handouts. If you are acting as a promotional product advisor,

then it is your job to encourage your customer to upgrade to polo shirts from basic tees.

Denim and Sweat Shirts

In addition to T-shirts, sweatshirts and hoodies are popular for school emblems. Just make sure your printer's ink volume setting is high. As we discussed in the previous chapter, some printers do not have ink level control, making it difficult for them to print on thicker fabrics such as sweatshirts. Garment printers also do an excellent job of printing on denim and jean materials, so make sure you have some good printed jean samples in the store and on your Web site. Printed jeans and jean shirts command higher prices than T-shirts, giving you a much higher margin.

Hoodie

Baby's Bibs

Short

B. Golf Shirts and Golf Towels

Many golf and country clubs need custom printed shirts and golf towels, but they may lack the volume to justify screen-printing. With digital apparel printing, these clubs can offer many more designs to their customers at low volume. When they hold tournaments or special charity games, they can order special golf shirts. Printing on golf shirts is essentially no different from printing polo shirts or T-shirts. For golf towels, make sure you use plenty of ink, just like on sweatshirts. You may consider specializing in golf shirt printing. Once you have several golf courses as clients, you can use them as references for other golf club businesses. Many courses are managed by the same management company, so it may be possible for you to get orders for dozens of golf clubs from the same company.

Golf Shirt and Towel

C. Polyester and Nylon Items

The direct-to-garment printers typically use water-based pigmented inks, which are suitable for cotton fabrics. Most of these inks will also work well with polycotton or cotton-polyester 50% blends. Many athletic wears, however, are made of micro-fiber, high performance or high tech 100% polyester, nylon or other man-made fabrics. The typical water-based inks will not work on these types of fabrics – they simply will not adhere to the fabric properly. Recently AnaJet started offering a special ink printing directly on synthetic fiber textile, which works well with 100% polyester and other man-made material. Such specialty inks are ideal for high-tech athletic wear made of synthetic fibers and 100% nylon tote bags favored by the promotional industry. We are not aware of any other makers of such inks. When you use such a specialty ink, test and test. The makers do not test all available fabrics, and new fabrics appear all the time. Sometimes what appears to be the same fabric does not work due to special coating applied to the fabric or garment. As the garment decorator, you must test print to see if the specialty ink works on the specific garment you want to print before you start volume printing.

Nylon Backpack

D. Pillowcases

Pillowcases that bear special messages, emblems or even photos of loved ones and pets are very popular. You may consider offering several varieties of pillowcases or pillows for custom printing. You can purchase polyurethane pillow cushion materials and pre-made blank pillowcases at wholesale for just a few dollars. You also may be able to find local seamstresses who will sew pillowcases using a special fabric that you can purchase at stores such as Joanne Fabrics, a nationwide chain.

Pillow Cases

E. Quilts

You can print photos and other custom images on pieces of fabric and make quilts from them. One store, www.portraitquilts.com, specializes in making photo quilts. It makes throw quilts, wall-hangings, bed spreads, pillow shams, pillow cases, quilted tote bags, etc. They take orders from retailers as well as end-user consumers. Visit the company's Web site—not so much to imitate the business model, but to start thinking about your own unique idea and business model.

Making quilts out of old T-shirts has become a popular hobby. Some books about T-shirt quilts and Web sites are listed below.[16]

http://quiltingbeez.com/TShirtQuilts.html
www.easyt-shirtquilt.com

F. Head Wear

You can offer baseball caps and other types of head wear, but these are somewhat difficult to print using a direct-to-garment printer. You need to use flat material on the print table; obviously, most headwear is not flat. Most of the hat adaptors offered by printer manufacturers to hold down hats generally do not work very well. Headwear printing takes time to mount the material. If you can find headwear that can be held or laid flat, then consider it.

There are some applications we would like to warn you about. They include printing on non-textile materials such as golf balls, ceramic items and metal pieces. Some direct-to-garment printer salespeople have promoted the ability to print on these items. A printer is a printer; therefore, a printer should be able to print on these items in addition to garments, they say.

But this is neither practical nor commercially viable. Well-performing direct-to-garment printer inks are optimized for printing on textile fabrics. A different type of ink is required to print on golf balls or ceramic items, notably a solvent-based ink. Besides, the substrates generally require pre- and post-coating to have any print longevity. If you have a cartridge-based printer, replacing one type of ink with another type is relatively simple; however, the ink remaining in the printer must be purged with a cleaning solution before the new ink is installed. This is time-consuming, and the cost of wasted ink and cleaning solution can be significant when you switch to a totally different family of ink.

If you have a printer that uses open ink containers, switching from one type of ink to another is rather daunting. With such machines, the entire ink delivery system essentially must be replaced and the print heads need to be cleaned. It is a time-consuming and expensive process during which the ink can become contaminated. Thus printing on golf balls and ceramics, while not impossible, is not practical. Golf balls can be printed efficiently by a pad printer, which sells for as little as $1,000. It makes little sense for anyone to tie up a more expensive direct-to-garment printer for these items. If you do your homework properly, you will have more business than you can handle by just printing on garments.

CHAPTER 9

Printing Decorative Art and Portrait Photos

Giclée is the process of inkjet printing fine art on canvas, a technique that produces art prints of very high quality. Inkjet printing of fine art is nothing new, but we never imagined that this might be another way to use a digital apparel printer. Paul Green, an Artist-in-Residence at AnaJet, played with this idea and came up with surprisingly good results. The Giclée printing of limited edition art is usually supervised and signed by the original artist. The decorative art reproduced on canvas by a direct-to-garment printer is not "real" Giclée printing, but are of such high quality that they resemble the original oil painting in full color.

The art print process begins with digital files of artwork. Remember that you must be careful about applicable copyright laws when you reproduce art. Generally, images of paintings by famous old masters such as Renoir, Rembrandt, Van Gogh or Degas are in the public domain, as long as they were produced many years ago. However, certain digital images of such fine art may have been copyrighted.

Decorative Art Prints with Oil Painting Effect

When you acquire a digital image, the seller should be able to indicate whether you need to pay a royalty for its reproduction. When the art is printed on an inkjet-receptive canvas and is coated with a protective finish like AnaJet Texture Coat^{TM}, the prints look just like an oil painting. Whether the original is an oil painting, watercolor, lithography or even portrait photography, the results can be stunning. The printed art can be sold at arts and crafts fairs, home decorating stores and other similar businesses. If you have a Web site, you can even sell the decorative art online. You no longer need to wait for custom shirt printing orders; you can now proactively engage in production work.

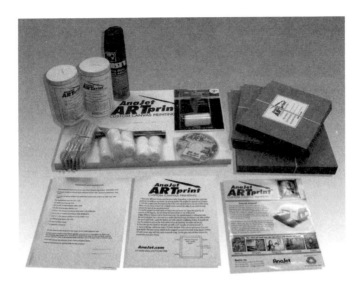

ARTprint™ Package

At AnaJet, we tell customers that they should never allow their printers to sit idle for lack of work. Whenever there is custom apparel printing to be done, the printer should do it. But when there are no custom jobs, the printer should print decorative art. The material cost of each print is just a few dollars, but the resulting decorative art can sell at a significantly higher price depending on the local market. AnaJet now offers a package known as ARTprint™, which consists of inkjet-receptive coated canvas, Texture Coat™, a CD containing royalty-free digital art compilations and a business development manual plus instructional video. This is a great way to reduce the uncertainty inherent in a start-up. Decorative art production is simply an additional way to generate revenue.

Portrait Print with Texture Coat™

Photography studios may charge several hundred dollars for a canvas reproduction of a portrait photography, but there are many ways of putting photo images on canvas. In fact, the ARTprint™ system is the most direct and least expensive way. Similar to art reproduction, the canvas reproduction of a portrait closely resembles an oil painting of the portrait. You should contact portrait photo studios and event photographers to offer your textured canvas photo service. Make sure you provide brochures and sample canvases, attractively framed. The portrait studio does not even have to be local.

CHAPTER 10

Photo Shirt Printing

P eople love to wear shirts printed with photos or likenesses of their loved ones – children, pets, or whatever they are passionate about. Such custom photo shirts represent a tremendous opportunity for digital apparel printers.

A leading market research firm, I.T. Strategies, conducted a survey in the spring of 2007. Of the 1,600 photographers who responded, exactly half showed interest in an inkjet printer that could print photographic images directly on finished garment.[17] But many were not familiar with the existence of such printer technology, and they had concerns about the image quality and durability of prints. Their dominant interest was in the opening up of a new market.

During the planning stage of this book, we did not intend to include this opportunity because no one was able to offer a commercially viable instant photo shirt system. Due to widely varying situations such as lighting conditions and the different skin tones of customers, most of the instant photos taken at a store require photo editing to enable printing at an acceptable level of quality. If the software is optimized for printing images of people with fair complexions, ethnic customers' images will print too dark. In the opposite setting, a blond with a very fair complexion will appear washed out. Capable photo editing software can handle this problem effectively, but such software is impractical for use at instant photo stores. When you go out shopping for such a system, demand to see a live demonstration during which people of various skin tones can be photographed instantly and printed without any photo editing. Any preprinted or prepackaged demonstration will not allow you to fully evaluate whether the system is commercially viable.

Photo Shirt with a Dropped-In Background

AnaJet engineers refined this technology so that it can be used in a store environment using only a point-and-shoot camera. One can print newly taken or old photos. But one of the most exciting applications is that of the AnaChroma™ program. Once digital photos are taken against a chroma key green screen, the AnaChroma™ program allows to drop in any photo or graphic image as the background. Using the program, you can also send the photo files to a private or public photo server via the Internet so that your associates can download them for printing. This means that the retail stores at which the photos are taken do not even need to have direct-to-garment printers. All they need is a digital camera, chroma key green screen, the AnaChroma™ program and a good Internet connection. This opens up many new possibilities for your business.

Suppose you have a direct-to-garment printer with an AnaChroma™ program. You can establish agreements with numerous retail stores that will take photographs of their customers. These can be uploaded to the photo server with one mouse click, along with the customer information. You can download the file, and print and ship the shirt to the customer. All you need to do is settle the account with the retail store. With this technology, you can now have dozens of retail outlets working for you. Such photo shirts are all one-of-a-kind custom items and the quantity is usually low. Thus, your retail outlets should be able to price them high enough to allow both them and you a good profit margin.

If you use a wireless SLR camera, such as the ones offered with AnaJet PHOTOshirts™ System, the commercial application will be even simpler. With such a system, there are no wires, cables, power cords or lighting needed for the store operation. These mundane issues can become significant problems at a store where space is limited and customers are in constant motion. The beauty of this process is that the skill level needed to take the pictures, run the computer and print the shirt is very low. Almost any worker can be trained to do the entire operation in 15 to 20 minutes.

ANAJET PHOTOSHIRT™ SYSTEM WITH WIRELESS CAMERA

| AnaJet wireless camera, with Chromakey green screen. | Photos appear on the monitor with no background. | Drop in any background with AnaChroma Program. | Send the photo file to the printer, locally or over internet for garment printing. | Heat treat with a heat press for finished product. |

The key element of PHOTOshirts™ is, of course, the customer's own picture. But the background image is also very important since it sets the tone for the decorated garment. At a shop in Las Vegas, it would be reasonable to expect that people would want their pictures adorned with scenes from Las Vegas; they might want to appear beside a showgirl, at a gaming table or before a landmark. In a Hawaiian location, people may want to appear in a beach scene or against Diamond Head.

For any hometown location, people might want their pictures set against backdrops such as exotic vacation spots, waterfalls, and mountains or next to celebrities. Some may want humorous backdrops such as: "WANTED $1,000,000 REWARD DEAD OR ALIVE," or "TIMES' PERSON OF THE YEAR." The AnaJet PHOTOshirts™ System comes with a collection of these backdrop images. If you are assembling images on your own, they do not need to be in any particular format or in a specific resolution. A pixel size of about 800 x 1000 or higher will do nicely for photo shirt printing.

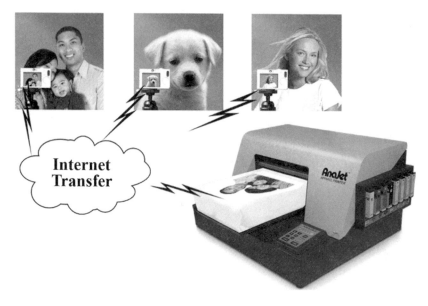

Many Satellite Stores can Generate Business for a Single Printer

CHAPTER 11

Sell, Sell, Sell

Considering that just one direct-to-garment printer is capable of producing several hundred thousand dollars worth of decorated end products, the key to success lies in the operator's ability to sell the printing service and printed items. If you choose a properly engineered printer, the production operation is relatively easy. There is also a well-developed supply chain of blank stocks on which you can print, including shirts, aprons, towels, canvas, mouse pads and so on. There aren't very many things that can complicate this business. Selling is the main business you need to concentrate on.

Is There Really a Market to Which I Can Sell?

From the 2007 study, we now know that garment decoration is a $44-billion industry in the U.S. Embroidered garments constitute only one fifth of this industry. More than $22 billion worth of printed garments are sold in the United States at the wholesale level; that is the value of printed garments received by the garment decorators. A good part of this market is open to any direct-to-garment printer. Inkjet printing, still a new technology, currently accounts for less than 1% of the total garment decoration industry. The potential market size and opportunities for direct-to-garment printers are indeed tremendous.

American garment decorators (all types) had an average (mean) revenue of $787,900 and 5 employees in 2006.[8] If you count only full-time garment decorators, the average shop's revenue was just over $1 million, generated by 7 employees. Full-time screen printing garment decorators had an average of $1.3 million revenue in 2006. Of course, these statistics are drawn from the experience of screen printers, who have considerably higher investments and longer operating history than digital printers. There are not enough digital printers to provide comparable statistics yet. Given that the direct-to-garment printer offers a greater advantage than screen printing in terms of run size flexibility, turnaround time, print quality and production cost, digital printers should not have much difficulty competing against garment decorators who use other types of printing methods.

So who are your customers? According to the 2007 study, local businesses represent the biggest customer group for garment decorators. About two-thirds are local companies. The implication is clear. Face-to-face sales will continue to be very important. The customer groups most frequently cited by garment decorators are local businesses, athletic teams, educational institutions, retailers, corporations and non-profits. Other less-cited but still important customer groups are government, construction trades, financial, health care, hospitality and professional firms. Other customers include promotional product distributors and other apparel decorators, i.e. embroiderers who source out garment printing. These latter two groups may be much more important than shown in this study. They may have been included in local businesses.

Although not directly related to digital apparel printing, the SGIA 2008 market strategies survey also shows where the garment decoration business comes from.[18] The survey reveals that the top markets for the garment decorators are: educational institutions, non-profits, athletic teams, corporate branding and retail businesses. The survey respondents are SGIA member firms, who use screen printing as their primary means of printing. It is unclear why the top five markets have shifted between 2007 and 2008, but we suspect it may be simply due to a small survey sample size. In any case, there is not much difference in importance between the first-place market and fifth-place market. All of the markets identified in the table should be considered important.

THE MOST IMPORTANT CUSTOMER GROUPS

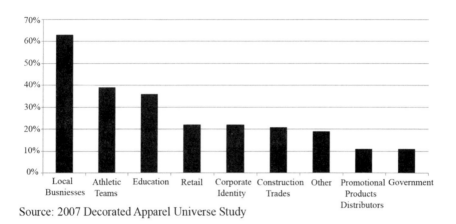

Source: 2007 Decorated Apparel Universe Study

THE TOP FIVE MARKETS FOR GARMENT DECORATORS

2008 Top Markets	2007 Top Markets
1. Educational Institutions	1. Athletic Teams
2. Non-Profits	2. Educational Institutions
3. Corporate Branding	3. Retail Business
4. Athletic Teams	4. Non-Profits
5. Retail Business	5. Corporate Branding

Source: SGIA

Sales and Marketing Go Hand In Hand

Relative to your current and potential customers, you have sales and you have marketing. If you conduct proper marketing, the sales will naturally follow. Most small business owners are afraid even to talk about marketing. But anyone can become a superb marketer without spending a lot of money, as we will show in the next chapter. You cannot generate a meaningful sales volume without it. By the same token, even if you are a good marketer, you still need effective sales efforts. These can be compared to the air and ground elements in a military campaign. Think of marketing as the broad coverage of air power that enables the ground troops to wield their sales efforts and conquer the territory. One is not effective without the other. Without marketing coverage, sales are hard to come by; without actual sales efforts, your superb marketing will be wasted.

Whether your shop is a startup or an already prosperous business, we suggest you devote at least 80% of your time to sales and marketing. If your business is just starting up, you don't have much else to do as of yet. When the orders do start to come in, you can devote as much time as necessary to print the shirts. But if you can afford it, you should hire someone to do the printing. You'll want to inspect the quality unless you have a production or quality manager, but you should not spend your valuable time printing shirts. Rather, as the business owner, you should spend your time to drum up new sales.

For that, you need some actionable plans. Don't wait for someone to call you —you certainly do not want to be passive. After all, you are an entre-preneur who wants to take control and make things happen. Therefore, you need to identify some likely or promising prospects. Once you find them, you will be sending fliers and emails, telephoning and visiting them. At the end of this chapter, we will discuss resellers who will act as your distributors and take orders for you.

Sending Brochures and Fliers

As you read in Chapter 4, How Others Have Found Success, it's likely that most of your customers are local, although digital apparel printing lends itself well to a nationwide customer base. Your initial sales efforts should strongly target local business customers. One of the most elementary sales efforts you can initiate is sending out sales brochures or fliers. Your brochures do not need to be fancy; they should simply look professional, tasteful and be infor-mative. If you are not a graphic designer, hire one. A 2- or 4-page offset color brochure will do. Refrain from producing these with your desktop printer or copier; leave this to the professionals. After all, your brochure is part of your marketing strategy and represents your business.

Look for a local designer who can take digital photos of your sample products and design your brochures for a reasonable price. If you have a tight budget, you might consider finding a graphic arts student on your local www.craigslist.com site. Students may do the job free for the experience or else charge a cut-rate fee. As your business grows and your advertising budget increases, you can hire professionals.

Whatever business services you need, get into the habit of using professionals —or at least a knowledgeable student. Your brochure designer may also be able to help you design the graphics for your garments.

If you would like to include a sales letter, you can write your own. If you need some help writing a direct mail sales letter, consult Web sites such as:

http://owl.english.purdue.edu/owl/resource/655/01/
www.instantsalesletters.com.

Mailing List Sources

You can get mailing lists from any number of sources. They range from free lists that you compile yourself to expensive list brokers.

- Yellow Pages: The most obvious and least expensive resource would be your local Yellow Pages or other telephone directories that list businesses by type. They also include addresses that you can copy onto your flier for mailing.
- Online Directories: www.yellowpages.com/, www.superpages.com/, and http://yp.yahoo.com. These are free online directories where you can get business names, addresses, phone numbers and Web sites. After you specify the location, they will list businesses in specific categories.
- Mailing List Brokers: Your local Yellow Pages will list those who rent mailing lists. Research "mailing list broker" in the Business-to-Business Yellow Pages.
- Magazines: Various trade magazines rent mailing lists of their subscribers as well as those in the same industry, even if they are not subscribers.
- Trade Associations and Chamber of Commerce: Trade Associations and Chambers of Commerce publish their member directories and often make them available either free or at nominal costs. Some do not rent them to non-members, while others may be available on the Internet.

Sending Emails

Sending emails to prospective customers is a great way to gain exposure at a reasonable cost —but be careful. There is a certain stigma attached to email marketing; many people associate even legitimate marketing emails with spam. Spam is sending out bulk email indiscriminately to recipients who don't want it. Not only is spam incapable of attracting any new business, it will also ruin your reputation.

Once you are labeled as a spammer, it is essentially a death sentence for any future email-based marketing efforts. It is very important to know the ins and outs of email marketing and use it judiciously. You will probably need outside help to implement a proper campaign. Check out the expert's reputation to assess his effectiveness —and make sure he does not use spam.

You may want to consider using inexpensive Web-based e-mail marketing services. Such Web sites also offer free basic lessons on e-mail marketing, and they may host user discussion boards where you can learn more from your peers.

Telephoning Prospects

Telephone calls to prospects can be one of the most powerful sales tools – if used correctly. Cold calls can waste a lot of your time, while calling those to whom you have already sent fliers or e-mails may open doors more easily. You may see immediate results or you may simply remind them of the availability of your service. This reinforces your other advertising campaigns. If you call, make a quick assessment of whether it will be worthwhile to follow up with an actual visit. In that case, ask for an appointment.

If you need some guidance on over-the-phone sales, there are many fine telephone sales training seminars and programs; you can also read up on the subject.[19]

Visiting Prospects

This is the most expensive method among many different ways of selling. However, it may be an important way to acquire business customers, particularly if you run a home-based business. Visit those companies that have responded to your ads, fliers, e-mails or phone calls. Bring along business cards, fliers, pricing schedules and assorted samples to give away. The samples should include your business name, Web site address and telephone number printed right on the shirts.

Targeting Prospects

Any business, organization, family or individual is a potential customer. However, the surveys show that local businesses, athletic teams, schools and retail shops are among the most likely customers for you. Naturally, these should become the focus of your efforts. Let's look at some of these targets.

Businesses and Corporations

This is probably your single most important target group. The Yellow Pages and local business directories are obvious easy starting points in identifying potential businesses that may need custom shirts. Most of them will order custom shirts featuring their company names, logos, products or brands at some point. They will also order custom shirts for employee uniforms, trade shows, special events, sporting events or just for team building.

The marketing or brand shirts will be the most profitable for you. The marketing departments will order logo or brand shirts to give to their best customers, their distributors or just to give away at trade shows. Companies will typically order such shirts when a new product line or a new marketing campaign is launched. Watch your local news sources to learn about such upcoming business activities. Contact these companies' marketing managers, brand managers or product managers.

Companies use brand shirts as walking advertisements. They cost much less than printed media or television ads and they deliver brand exposure to the public. Free or low-cost brand shirts are particularly effective when distributed to dealership sales and service crews. These free shirts will gain the goodwill of recipients who are basically the foot soldiers that move their company products. In addition, when the dealer crews wear brand shirts, the brand gets significant exposure at the most auspicious occasions. Do not assume these marketing managers know all about the power of promotional products. Later in this book, we devote a chapter how you can train yourself as a promotional product advisor to assist your clients and increase your sales.

Companies will also order logo or branded shirts for their own employees, as daily wear and particularly at trade shows. These shirts are typically polo shirts as opposed to T-shirts, of higher quality than those they simply give away. However, some businesses, particularly those that include blue-collar workers or less formal business cultures, still prefer T-shirts. Special events, such as company anniversaries, training programs, new marketing campaigns, new product launches, team building efforts, or corporate athletics, are all excellent occasions for customized company shirts. Contact the purchasing departments, sales managers or special events or sporting directors for these opportunities.

Once you get in with a corporation, milk every opportunity. When a manager is happy with your products and services, ask him to introduce you to other managers who may also order customized apparel. If you cannot produce what he needs, refer him to another high-quality decorator — preferably one that is not competing with you.

This is one reason why you need alliances with reliable embroidery houses and screen printers. If a purchaser specifically asks that logos be embroidered, you can still take the order and have your buddy's embroidery house do the job. If the graphic is simple and a large quantity of shirts you cannot handle is ordered, farm it out to a screen printer. There will be a sufficient margin for both of you. But the main point is that the client will remember you and call you whenever they need more company shirts. For corporate buyers, price is not usually the highest priority. Quality, timely delivery and a trouble-free relationship with the vendor—you—are the most important factors. For most companies, your ability to reproduce their logo and company colors accurately is vital. Keep this in mind during production.

Local Athletic Teams

Local baseball, football, softball, basketball and soccer teams as well as little leagues, school teams and cheering teams can be found in almost every community. Tees, sweatshirts, hoodies, jerseys, warm-up gear and even socks can have logos. We know of several digital apparel printers who got started with their own kids' little league or softball teams. Once you start printing shirts for one team, you can easily make your capability known to other teams in the league.

Schools

Most schools have activities that require team uniforms or shirts imprinted with the school emblems and activity graphics. You can start by calling all of the school athletic departments and bookstores. If you have a Web site, you can post pictures of various garments embellished with local school emblems. Make sure you conform to the rules relating to the use of school emblems by inquiring of school officials. This may open up a new relationship with the school for future decorated garment orders.

Retail Stores and Clothing Stores

Today, many retail and clothing stores offer their own unique T-shirts with special graphics of their own design. These special shirts are not available anywhere else and they usually demand premium prices. Often, they do not have enough volume to order hundreds of shirts from a screen printer, or their designs are too complex to screen print. As a digital apparel printer, you would be ideally suited to cater to the needs of these shops. If you can provide the garment graphic design service, let them know that you offer a wraparound service. They will also appreciate your re-labeling service. Essentially, you are offering one-stop shopping. When the shirts become successful, you will have locked in a lucrative relationship.

Churches and Church Groups

Many churches host significant numbers of organized activities. Special youth schools, missionary tours, family events, summer bible schools, nurturing and retreat events, prayer events, fundraising events, sporting events etc. are all occasions that call for team shirts. If you go to a church, you can start there. Make fliers especially designed for churches and mail them out. Actually, they may even have volunteer graphic designers that you might recruit for your own business.

Health Clubs and Sporting Clubs

Many health and sporting club members like to wear club T-shirts. Most clubs have pro shops that sell workout clothes, swimsuits and athletic shoes. All of these shops are potentially good clients. Many smaller clubs without such shops still sell club T-shirts at their reception counters. Since most health clubs probably cannot order a large enough quantity to interest a screen printer, your digital apparel printer short run service may come in handy for them.

Restaurants

One of our doctor friends owns an upscale seafood restaurant in California, and he was very interested in purchasing an AnaJet printer. His idea was to take pictures of waiting customers during busy times and print custom photo T-shirts beneath his restaurant logo. He thought he could make good money while amusing hungry customers who were waiting for tables —sometimes for as long as two hours on weekend evenings. We talked him out of it since we did not think he would have enough customers to justify the machine during such limited hours of operation. Because he heeded our advice, we won't know if his idea would have worked —but he can certainly sell pre-printed shirts adorned with his restaurant emblem. Better yet, he can take pictures of customers for photo shirts to be completed the next day using systems like AnaJet PHOTOshirts™. He can do so by contracting with a printer operator —someone like you.

You can approach every restaurant in your city to propose a similar operation. We learned that patrons love to buy and wear T-shirts featuring their favorite restaurants. Restaurants that carry their own branded T-shirts get free advertising when their patrons wear these in public. So the shirts can nurture a loyal customer base and act as free ads.

You should approach just about every restaurant in your city for logo shirts, except for fast food joints and low-end eateries. Some may even go for the photo T-shirt idea. Offer to print the first order of 25 shirts and increase the quantity to 50 once they sell out. For those who don't get it, explain that this is truly killing two birds with one stone. They not only make money by selling the shirts, but also they get free advertisements and nurture loyal patrons. See if you can persuade them to give away free shirts to regular or important customers.

Hotels

Many hotels, particularly resorts, have their own logo shirts available in their gift shops. We have seen smaller hotels that lack gift shops displaying their logo shirts at the front desk on a display rack. They also often carry shirts featuring local scenes or the name of the town. Their required quantity often is not large enough to get them screen printed. This can present an excellent opportunity for you. People staying at hotels are mostly out-of-towners and they are likely to buy shirts as mementos, gifts or for workouts.

Fundraising Organization and Events

Various cancer societies, charitable organizations and groups like hospital affiliates, foundations, ad-hoc organizations, etc. are always organizing events for fundraising purposes. Look for them in local directories and newspapers. Most of these events include decorated garments. Imprinted T-shirts for sporting activities and outdoor events, like 10Ks and 5Ks, are particularly popular. These events offer excellent opportunities for you to network while contributing to a good cause. You may even want to become a sponsor and offer your decorated garments free or at cut-rate prices that are just high enough to recover your costs. Most event organizers are very conscious of providing publicity to their sponsors. Your good deeds will be amply rewarded.

Election Campaigns

Election campaigns are now some of the most lavishly spending organizations. Whether it is for the presidential, congressional or local election, it may be worth your efforts to contact various election campaign offices to solicit their business. They order various printed garments to sell, give to volunteers or for fund raising. We read some of the '08 Obama presidential campaign limited edition T-shirts given to the attendees of a fundraising event would turn up in eBay fetching more than $1,000.

Election Campaign Shirts

Public Television and Radio Stations

Public television and radio stations rely to some extent on fundraising to defray their operating expenses. Many also have online or brick-and-mortar stores. Both the stores and fundraising drives may need your printing services. T-shirts printed with radio station logos have special appeal as donor gifts. It's a new option and an alternative to the common music CDs and DVDs. And the station and donors get the same benefits as did the previously mentioned restaurant and patrons. Don't hesitate to make your pitch to the station managers, as you do to the restaurant managers, regarding the benefits brought by logo shirts. If your finances allow, you may want to make a tax-deductible donation of 25 shirts to your local public radio station each time it conducts a drive. These stations are usually conscientious about recognizing your donation, which will generate further publicity.

There is no reason to limit your contacts to local stations, though you will likely start your business there. Once you develop a working relationship with one or two local stations, consider going nationwide if your resources permit. For local stations, you may not only send fliers, you might also choose to call and visit. For stations outside your immediate area, send fliers to introduce yourself. Indeed, they may surprise you by being the first to call.

Others

There are many other potential customers within your community. The following are some examples.

- Health and organic food stores
- Grocery stores
- General and hardware stores
- Pet shops
- Festivals
- Special Event Organizers
- Real estate agencies
- Bowling alleys
- Spas
- Beauty and hair salons
- Chambers of Commerce and convention and visitors bureaus
- City and various other government agencies, particularly parks, beach and youth programs and social services departments.
- Police and fire departments

RESELLER PROGRAM

Resellers are those clients who will take imprinted garment orders from their customers and have you do the printing for them. You will typically charge resellers 30 to 35 percent less than your direct customers; therefore, your margin will be less. However, these resellers are very valuable to you for several reasons.

Their orders are steady wholesale orders and they are doing all the sales and marketing work for you. Since they are in the trade, they usually have excellent business sense and will not take up a great deal of your time, thus reducing your "soft costs" —the customer service cost. Once you develop a good working relationship, they will place repeat orders with you. Finally and most importantly, resellers can serve as your market intelligence agents. They can feed you information about what goes on in the garment decoration industry, including what customers are currently looking for and what are the latest trends.

Consider your resellers a very important part of your sales and marketing program. You should implement a reseller program as soon as possible. You need to show them that your service will enhance their business, provide convenience to their customers and increase their margins as well. Suppose you have 20 resellers. If each places just one order per week, your reseller program generates 1,000 orders per year (20 outlets x 50 weeks). If each order is for 25 shirts, it amounts to 25,000 shirts per year, or 250,000 shirts over a ten-year period. This is a serious business volume, and you can earn it if you can execute the program.

You must be well prepared before approaching potential resellers. They are established businesses, while you are just starting out. Still, you are the leader to whom they will look for guidance. As a result, you must develop a complete and professional-looking reseller package that should include the following elements.

- **Product Catalog**: Don't make it complicated. Offer no more than two or three dozen blank shirts and other product options. Professional-looking photos of products are a must, and you may be able to get them from the shirt manufacturers' Web sites. Otherwise, have the photographs taken by a professional. Specify in the catalog the graphics file format you can accept, the method of specifying the location of graphics and the available text fonts.

- **Price List:** Cross-referencing your product catalog will allow you to show the price you intend to charge your reseller and the recommended price they should charge their customers. Prices should be based on the product and quantity. Keep the list as simple as possible. Offer prices in brackets of, for example 1-2 pieces, up to 25 pieces, up to 50 pieces and over 50 pieces, etc. By simplifying the pricing scheme, you make it easy for your resellers do business with you. Remember that they may not have anyone who is trained in how to handle your products. Some sales clerks will need to improvise, and they will need to be able to rely on the clarity and completeness of your price list.

- **Sample Shirt Board:** For each garment category, provide one attractively printed sample. You do not need to provide more than half a dozen. If you can afford it, fix them on a 3-foot x 5-foot rigid backboard the resellers can hang on a wall. These sample boards will become your silent sales force. This can be your most solid investment if you choose the right resellers. You may have to offer these sample boards free, but determine whether you can have them pay for the actual cost of the sample boards.

- **Point of Purchase Display Board:** Print a simple point of purchase (POP) display board. You may need to work with a sign shop or digital printing shop to prepare the POP displays. Make them eye-catching but simple. Emphasize the quality of print and your quick turnaround, not your low price.

- **Operating Guidelines and Order Sheet**: The order sheet should include all the information you need to produce the ordered shirts. Also, provide clearly written and itemized information sheets of no more than 1-2 pages. With this informational sheet, you will guide the reseller's clerks on how they should take orders, offer them some sales tips and contact information. You may also include frequently asked questions. Remember, their sales clerks are going to read this information while their customers are waiting. As a result, it needs to be well-organized and concise.

Here are some resellers that may be interested in customized printed shirts. Do not get discouraged if the first five shops you approach turn you down. This may simply be because you are not presenting the proposal correctly. Keep at it and evaluate why they do not sign up with you. Eventually, as you improve your presentation and business model, you will find some takers. Every time you are turned down, remind yourself that you are working on a quarter-million shirt project. As soon as you have a few satisfied resellers, you will have references and it will get progressively easier to sign up more resellers.

Screen-printing Shops: As we have stated frequently, screen printers cannot handle short runs, full color, complex graphics, photo printing or orders that must be filled the same or the next day.

However, since screen printers are in the garment printing business, they are your best allies. Convince them to work with you. Many large shops may not bother to become your reseller, but might just refer customers to you. That's even better. Leave a handful of your business cards with them, and make sure to visit regularly so that you can leave simple gifts and replenish your business cards. You should reciprocate by referring customers who need thousands of shirts with very simple single-color graphics. Such customers will not want to pay your price, and screen printers with automatic screens can do the job more efficiently. Having such a reciprocal customer referral program will cost you very little, but it can be an important resource for your business.

Embroidery Shops: Linking up with your local embroidery shops should be high on your priority list. Embroidery is "the other method" of garment decoration. Many embroidery and monogram customers need to order printed shirts. Most embroidery shops farm out the printing function to screen printing shops. When the order is for a small run, requires complex or full color graphics, your digital apparel printing is a natural choice. An increasing number of embroiderers now offer mixed media decoration, which incorporates your printing with their embroidery. Like screen printers, some embroidery shops may refer their customers to you for printing jobs. Be aware that in the U.S., over 40 percent of all embroidery shops are home-based businesses and are generally smaller than screen printing shops. Always sustain a good relationship with reciprocation.

Promotional Product Distributors: Advertising specialty or promotional products is one of the world's fastest-growing industries. An important part of this business is custom-printed textiles such as T-shirts, aprons, polo shirts, golf shirts and golf towels. Mouse pads are another important item. The majority of these distributors will contract out the textile imprinting to garment decoration shops. Since most of their orders are for less than 250 pieces, your digital apparel printing is more suitable than screen printing for them. They will be extremely happy that you can provide the imprinting service for any quantity of shirts. There are over 30,000 such distributors in the United States. Most of them, even the small operators, will take orders from a nationwide client base. Likewise, the operators do not have to be local. Once you take orders, you can fulfill them by drop-shipping the shirts to the customer or by shipping to the promotional product distributor. Many of these businesses operate online stores, and you will need to provide a wider variety of shirt stocks that you can choose from your blank shirt supplier's site.

Sign Makers and Digital Printers: These are natural outlets for you. Since imprinted logo shirts represent a form of advertising, a surprising number of customers call sign shops to have their garments printed. The common notion that sign makers usually have screen printing machines may have something to do with this behavior. The truth is, machines used by sign makers are intended for solid surface printing and do not render well for garment printing. AnaJet has sold a considerable number of garment printers to sign shops, but most sign makers do not have garment printing capability and can become your resellers. The same goes with digital printers. They usually have roll-to-roll large format digital printers for graphics, sign and banner printing. Many of them will be interested in becoming your resellers.

Custom T-shirt Stores: In most U.S. towns, particularly those in resort areas, you will find many T-shirt stores that make custom shirts with heat-applied graphics. The customization may be made with preprinted graphics and text transfer sheets, graphics printed with laser printers, dye sublimation ink, cut twills or heat-applied vinyl. Each of these methods has drawbacks and limitations. Dye sublimation requires transfer only to polyester shirts, which are too warm for anyone's comfort. Nothing can match direct-to-garment printed 100% cotton shirts with vibrant, multi-color custom graphics. Many of these stores are small operators and have little in the way of related equipment or investment. You can contact them and offer a direct-to-garment printing reseller opportunity. Many of them will be glad to add your capability to their array of services without extra investment.

Clothing and T-shirt Shops: Most cities have dozens of T-shirt stores. With few exceptions, these businesses sell a variety of preprinted shirts but don't offer customized shirts. These merchants are interested in moving items but are not typically geared to provide the on-site services necessary for customization. Many of these will be glad to join up with you so that they can offer a custom shirt service—with you doing all of that service work.

Quick Printing Shops: Many people think of quick printing shops when they think of custom graphic printing of apparel. After all, it's a natural fit. Therefore, visit these independent or franchised quick printing shops and encourage them to carry your service. Many also have graphic designers on-site for clients. They can become value-added resellers with particularly with their graphic design services.

Photo Processing and Photo Print Shops: Some of these shops offer to print photos on items such as mugs, plates, tiles and mouse pads. Few offer to print photos on T-shirts, pillowcases, aprons and other textile materials. You may be one of the first to offer them such a service.

Personalization Shops: In most cities, you can find shops that offer personalization services on items such as jewelry, mugs, plaques and watches. As a result, offering them the opportunity to also provide personalized apparel, aprons, mouse pads or golf towels may be mutually beneficial. In fact, many of these businesses offer personalized embroidered apparel, but not printed apparel due to the nature of screen printing.

Trophy and Engraving Shops: Trophy shops typically offer engraving services on their trophies. They also offer many personalized engraved items and have access to customers who organize special events such as golf tournaments and other sporting activities. Many of their customers are good candidates for personalized or custom apparel.

Gift Shops: Personalized shirts, aprons, golf towels and pillow-cases make great gifts for birthdays, anniversaries, graduations, Valentine's Day, Halloween, Christmas, Mothers Day, Fathers Day, Prom—you name it. A gift shop's strength depends largely on the diversity of products it offers. You can help add to that diversity.

Fabric and Arts and Crafts Stores: People interested in arts and crafts or designing clothing frequent these shops to purchase their supplies. These people often design special apparel as a part of their own lines of clothing or under special commission from their clients. They will remember where they can get their designs printed and they will also become your clients.

Party Stores: Whether the occasion is a birthday party, class reunion or Halloween, party stores are great outlets for your personalized shirts. Befriend the managers to offer your personalized costume service. They will generate a steady flow or orders.

Wedding Stores and Wedding Coordinators: Surely, no one wears T-shirts at a wedding. But brides and grooms, as well as wedding coordinators, are looking for unique gift items. They like to present gifts to members of the wedding party, friends and family. They may include personalized items such as hankies, aprons, polo shirts, golf shirts or golf towels. You can imprint these gift items with special messages. We have also heard of at least one wedding where the bride and groom presented T-shirts adorned with their photos to all the guests.

Hardware Stores: People, particularly homeowners, go to hardware stores all the time. Many of these businesses are still owned by individuals who are actively looking for ways to counter the competition of the big-box stores. You may be able to persuade them to carry your shirts. When people see your printed shirt samples hanging at the entrance of a store, they will remember it when they have a need to print custom shirts.

CHAPTER 12

Marketing

We all know that marketing is the key to sales, and ultimately business success. For most small business owners, however, marketing is an overwhelming concept. The American Marketing Association defines marketing as "the activity, set of institutions, and processes for creating, communicating, delivering and exchanging offerings that have value for customers, clients, partners and society at large." It's certainly a mouthful, but you get the idea. Determining your business model, such as what you would sell to what kind of customers and by what method, is a part of the core of marketing. The other part is making existing and prospective customers understand the benefits of doing business with and trusting you. Sales will follow. It's that simple.

Marketing touches just about everything you do. Below, we will consider some of the marketing ideas tailored to a small business like yours – particularly in its early stages. It begins with the selection of your business name, how you answer your phone and how your Web site functions. It continues by addressing how you advertise, address your identity, price your product and control quality. All of these contribute to your communications with customers. Marketing does not need to cost a bundle; in fact, most of the elementary ideas we present here will cost you little or nothing at all.

Business Name and Internet Domain Name

It should be simple —easy to pronounce and remember. If possible, let it describe what you do best so that it will also convey your identity or market position. Associating your name with the name of the business tends to enhance credibility. But it should have flair. James Johnson Industries is not a particularly catchy name for a T-shirt printing shop. But JJ's Creative Tees says a lot if you offer a creative graphic design service as well. Two-Day Custom Tees may be a good one if your motto is a quick, two-day turn-around. Remember, though, in most parts of the country you need to register your business name as a fictitious business name or DBA (doing business as) name unless you are incorporated.

Make sure the business name you select is not in use by someone else or trademarked. More importantly, make sure you can get an Internet domain name under that business name. As a practical consideration, you may want to start researching available domain names before you fix on the name of your new business. Your Web site is going to be a powerful marketing tool, and you want your business name and Web site address to be the same or very similar. Since many domain names are hoarded by merchants, you may have a hard time coming up with a domain name you can use. If you do not know what a domain name is, refer to Chapter 14, Web Site Operation and Promotion.

In the above example, twodaytees.com, twodaycustomtees.com and 2daytees.com were available at the time of this writing; of course, they may be gone by the time you read this. A short and snappy Web site domain name is very important to any business. Some of the most successful T-shirt Web sites do not even offer a hint about what they do. For example, check out cafepress.com or zazzle.com.

Your Logo

Along with your business name, your logo is going to play an important role in branding your business. People who are visually stimulated by a logo will remember you better and will hopefully become repeat customers. So have a business logo designed for you. Use it on every possible occasion, on every page of your Web site, in your letterhead, business cards, invoices and on all printed sales materials. Imprint your logo on the shirt bags or shipping boxes if you have them manufactured for you. Make sure your logo appears in your store sign if you have a shop. Your logo should be clean, simple and distinctive, and it should use only one, two or three strong colors for easy reproduction.

Positioning

The positioning of your business in the market place is an important concept. Forget about being all things to all people. The market is just too big for any one business. To be successful, you must decide which market niche you want to serve. Otherwise, you will be lost in the market —be it low-end, high-end, low-priced, best service, fast turnaround, creative design assistance or large selection of apparel. Whatever the niche, you must position your business so that potential customers will know your identity and understand what they can expect from you. Just be aware of your own abilities; the combination of low price/ highest quality or quick turnaround/ large stock selection will not work for you. Study your market, evaluate your strength, then position yourself accordingly —and prominently —in the market. It's important to select your niche early on and include it in your business name. If you cannot make up your mind now, you can determine your positioning later. But the sooner you decide on your niche, the clearer your business direction will be.

Identity

Identity is what you are. It has a great deal to do with your abilities, your strengths, weaknesses, and the resulting market position you have taken. Be honest with yourself and represent your business as it truly is. That is your identity. Do not pretend to be something you are not, i.e., displaying the façade of a big corporation when you are actually a one- or two-man operation. Customers immediately will be alarmed and turned off if you deviate from your identity.

The elements you might consider negatives —such as a small operation, home-based business, high price or an inability to provide graphic services —can be positives if they are in line with your identity. If you run a home-based business, be proud! Remember, half of all businesses in the U.S. are home-based and they are thriving.

Pricing

We all know that low prices are a powerful marketing tool that generates sales. Some people argue that "high quality and low price" is the recipe for success. Indeed, it is a dream combination, but you simply may not be able to offer it, at least for now. We are all for high-quality, but not necessarily low price. Remember that your objective is to build a profitable business, not just to ring up sales. You must avoid unprofitable sales due to low prices, unless such transactions are part of your planned customer-building activities.

Many research reports show that quality, timely delivery, service, accuracy and value are much more important to customers than low price. With the exception of very special business models that build an identity based on the lowest price in the market, the notion of price is not that important. If you are just starting out or are still small, you probably cannot offer lower prices. Your low overhead probably is not a big enough factor. Low prices can be sustained only when you have a high volume operation backed by a huge investment and automation. But still, everyone wants to have a good deal, so be prepared to offer promotional prices —occasionally.

Repeat Business

Since most of your customers will be other businesses, getting repeat business is very important. How do you do this? You must provide high quality and good service to your clients, or else you will not receive repeat business. Your marketing efforts will get you the first order, but high-quality and conscientious customer service is what will get you the second order and beyond. Always consider quality and customer service as parts of your marketing program.

Branding

Since repeat customers are so important, you should make a concerted effort to brand your business so that customers and local businesses will remember you once they need decorated garments. Everything you do is related to branding. Some of the most important elements in your branding include product and service differentiation, catalogues and all types of sales literatures, logo-imprinted business shirts, and professional-looking business cards. You may include your logo and a tag line in invoices, order forms

– even packing tapes and shipping boxes. Moreover, it is important that you be visible at community activities. Become a member of your local chamber of commerce and participate in charity events. Do not pass up any opportunity to let locals know who you are. You want to be remembered as "the go-to guy (or gal)" for printing shirts.

Selection

For any apparel-related business, selection is very important. The ability to offer a wide variety of blank stock can be a cornerstone of your success. But the cost of implementing a wide selection is high. Increased selection means greater chances of mistakes and fouling up a simple operation. Fortunately, blank sportswear manufacturing and distribution are high-volume and highly competitive industries. They have a great deal of diversity and many offer wide selections through their Internet sites and telephone order desks. Most blank stocks can be delivered to your door within a day or two in small quantities. You will have to balance between the cost and complexity of offering a good selection and the simplicity of limited selection at great efficiency. The Appendix has a list of blank sportswear distributors and other blank stock wholesalers.

You also may want to study their product offerings online and in their catalogues, or even visit some of their showrooms. In most metropolitan areas, you can find half a dozen such showrooms. Talk to the sales managers there about what types of sportswear, what styles and which colors are in high demand. Fashion is a rapidly changing industry and you need to update your knowledge as much as possible through a near-continuous exchange of ideas with your professional colleagues.

Internet Web Site Operation

Your business Web site is so fundamentally important that we devoted an entire chapter to it. This is not so much about conducting business over the Net as it is to provide information to your customers. When the Web site looks orderly, informative and professional, people tend to trust the business. As mentioned previously, you can list all of your blank shirt stocks and other blanks, and include good product photos. You may also consider posting your production equipment list, photos of printers and other equipment, or possibly show a video of how your shirts are printed. All this increases the credibility of your business and enhances customer trust.

Email Marketing

In addition to the e-mail sales campaign we discussed in the previous chapter, you may also consider sending regular informative emails that relate to your garment decoration ideas and any expanded services you may offer. This might be particularly useful to your resellers and reseller candidates. Corporate marketing departments may want to know the latest news about decorated garment technology and services. You can collect the e-mails from your Web site or use existing customers' emails, but make sure you have the recipients' permission to re-send those emails. Many of your former customers will be glad to hear from you, and they will remember you the next time they need to have shirts printed. Over time, the e-mail list you compile will become one of your most valuable assets.

Advertising

There is no doubt that advertising can be an effective means of informing your potential customers about your service. But advertising is expensive, and measurements of their effectiveness are elusive. The direct mail of your fliers, as discussed, will be the most focused and effective method, but you may want to experiment with small advertisements in specialized media if your budget allows. Make sure you have a plan and an angle to drive your message to the targeted audience. Using media for the general public, such as daily newspapers, will not be suitable and will simply waste your money. When you finally develop a specific niche, advertise only in specialized media with appropriately focused audiences.

Networking

Attending networking meetings is an effective way of connecting with other businesses on a local level. At most networking meetings, attendees are typically given about 30 seconds to pitch their businesses. Afterwards, they have the opportunity to meet and mingle. Because your product cost is negligible, consider handing out shirts printed with your logo to fellow attendees. Find these business networking meetings through your local publications and attend as many B2B conferences as you can. The time you spend doing so will be well rewarded since you may obtain leads, referrals and customers. A secondary benefit is that you'll feel camaraderie and be inspired as you meet with other entrepreneurs. You will also learn many new ideas about how to promote and run your business.

The usual networking meetings are open to the public and cost little more than the price of your own breakfast. Some people prefer membership-based networking organizations. One of those is LeTip (www.letip.com), which operates 650 local chapters in the U.S. and Canada. Check the LeTip Web site for your local chapter, but be aware that you will not find this organization in every state. Another networking organization is BNI (www.bni.com), which claims to be the world's largest business networking organization with a presence in 40 countries. Membership in both of these organizations is pricey and members are encouraged to recruit new members and generate referrals. Despite such requirements, some business professionals prefer their formality and emphasis on higher levels of activity and regular interaction.

General networking sites, such as www.meetup.com, allow you to find local B2B networking meetings. Be careful in selecting networking groups, since many can simply be a waste of your time. Make certain that you perceive a good professional fit within the network; find people whose professions complement yours, including printers, digital printers, sign makers, event planners and marketers. If you've trained yourself to be an effective advisor in the use of promotional products, represent yourself as a promotional and marketing professional rather than as a garment decorator. Then, you will have become a business solution expert rather than a mere service provider.

Many of the methods presented in this chapter do not demand large investments, and they can be implemented easily. In fact, most are matters of attitude and the approach you take. There are many other marketing tools you can use, and we suggest you to read a book or two on small business marketing. One such book we can recommend is Ultimate Small Business Marketing Guide by James Stephenson.[20]

CHAPTER 13

Navigating Promotional Apparel Industry Successfully

A s we discussed in Chapter Three, the promotional apparel market provides fertile ground for direct-to-garment printers. Promotional apparel printing, with a typical run size of 25 to 250 pieces, is ideal for digital apparel printing. The colorful graphics and logos preferred by marketing departments can easily be done by the direct-to-garment printer, unlike screen-printing. Companies are typically in a hurry and cannot wait for a long lead time. Since you don't need to prepare silk screens, your ability to respond quickly will give you an advantage.

The 2007 decorated garment industry study showed that among full-time promotional garment distributors:

- 88% said they were more profitable or at least as profitable as the previous year;
- 9% said they were less profitable;
- 1% said they were not profitable.[8]

It's encouraging to see that nearly all promotional apparel distributors are profitable, whether they decorate the garments in-house or send them out. One will have to be very incompetent, negligent or both to belong to the bottom 1% that are not profitable.

According to the Advertising Specialty Institute (ASI), the promotional product industry had revenues of $19.6 billion in the U.S. in 2007.[12] Estimates from the Promotional Products Association International (PPAI), the industry's trade organization, are very similar.[14] The industry grew at a compounded annual rate of 4.7% over the last five years. In 2007, the industry grew 5.4% compared to the overall U.S. economic growth of 2.2%. The promotional product market is 83% larger than all radio ads and 73% larger than all Internet display ads. Digital apparel printers should seriously consider a focus on the promotional products industry.

PROMOTIONAL PRODUCTS INDUSTRY REVENUE GROWTH US TOTAL IN $BILLION

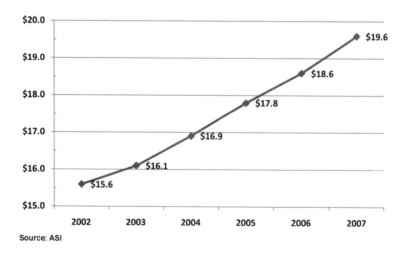

Source: ASI

PPAI broke down the 2006 industry sales figures by product category.[14] The top five product categories during that year were:

Wearables (Apparel)	30.78 %
Writing Instruments (Pens)	9.95 %
Calendars	6.47 %
Desk/Office Accessories	6.28 %
Bags	5.81 %

If you are a typical American consumer, you probably received at least one or more of these promotional items from a business within the last year. Today, the industry rule of thumb is that, by dollar value, about one-third of total promotional products are apparel or wearables. The most popular wearables are T-shirts, golf shirts, aprons, uniforms, hats and headbands, in that order. Of the $19.6 billion revenue of the promotional product industry in 2006, $5.7 billion was for promotional T-shirts and other apparel at the wholesale level — that is, the cost of shirts changing hands from suppliers or manufacturers, to distributors. At this level, most shirts are still blanks that have yet to be embellished.

The authors calculate that by the time company logos and marketing messages are imprinted, the value of promotional apparel reaches approximately $14.25 billion in the U.S.[9] This is fairly close to the survey results seen in the 2007 Decorated Apparel Universe Study, which estimated the total value of printed garments sold by promotional product distributors to be $13.1 billion.[8] An interesting observation is that, according to an ASI survey, less than 25% of promotional apparel suppliers (blank shirt manufacturers and wholesalers) provide any type of embellishment service. When they offer the service, they are limited primarily to embroidery, sparkles and studs. Few seem to offer a printing service, as blank apparel suppliers do not wish to compete with garment printers.

According to the 2007 study, 42% of promotional product distributors are home-based businesses, and about 60% decorate their garments in-house. We suspect that much of this in-house decoration is done by shops in industrial or commercial settings. Some home-based businesses may run simple embroidery machines. Most home-based promotional product distributors are not able to run screen printing equipment because of the toxicity of screen printing paste, noise and wastewater clean up. If they wish to decorate their garments in-house, direct-to-garment printing is the most ideal approach.

Whatever your current level of involvement with a promotional product business, a direct-to-garment printer should be an important part of your business strategy. According to the authors' calculations, the profit margin you can realize by printing in-house is roughly twice that of outsourcing the printing. You can also respond to customers' specific needs better when you have an in-house production capability and provide a much faster turn-around time than a screen printer. Quick and timely delivery of products are the top requirements for promotional product buyers. Price is secondary.

Promotional Wear Advisor

All promotional apparel distributors are different. To excel in this business, you need to distinguish yourself from others by creating value for clients. You should become an expert in the effective use of promotional wear by learning basic marketing principles and understanding how to design a promotional wear program. Doing so will lead to effective and measurable results with the promotional wear you provide. By becoming a promotional wear advisor or consultant to corporate clients, you will not have to compete on price, and the client will be locked in as your repeat customer. It does not require a great deal of effort to self-train as an effective promotional wear advisor. Once you do, your only concern will be how to expand your production ability, not your lack of sales or competition.

In fact, the most successful promotional product distributors operate as sales and marketing professionals. Since many of them subcontract their apparel decoration, you may have the opportunity to receive orders from fellow promotional product distributors if you have a production facility in-house. The ability to produce decorated apparel in-house will give you a distinct advantage over other promotional product distributors or garment screen printers.

When a T-shirt imprinted with a company's brand name or advertisement is given, the wearer becomes a walking billboard. A typical T-shirt will be worn an average of 50 times. If the wearer of the shirt is exposed to 20 people during the course of a day, the promo T-shirt brand ad can be viewed as many as 1,000 times during the life of the shirt. For both online and print ads, the advertising and publishing industries use a concept called CPM or cost per mille. That is the cost of an advertisement being viewed 1,000 times, or the cost per 1,000 impressions. According to this analysis, a promo T-shirt ad CPM is only $15 per 1,000 impressions, assuming the company pays $15 per shirt. The CPM for Internet display or banner ads is typically between $30 and $45, and these internet ads often must compete with a number of other ads on the same page. Printed media ad CPM is even more expensive. By any measure, the promotional T-shirt is a very cost effective form of advertising. In addition, you gain immeasurable goodwill from the wearers of the shirts. It becomes easy to argue in favor of promotional apparel. Many marketing managers are simply unaware of the benefits and effectiveness of promo wear as an advertising medium.

Here are some basic concepts relating to your training as a promotional wear expert. First, promotional products are not just freebies, handouts or giveaways. They must strongly improve the company's marketing program and generate both solid leads and sales. Like other marketing programs, if the results are measurable, the more valuable the promotional wear program will be. Let's consider an example in which the promotional product budget is wasted versus being utilized effectively.

Suppose a Mercedes-Benz automobile dealer plans to use promotional T-shirts with the MBZ logo. Mailing the shirts to prospects or giving them away to visitors may generate some goodwill, but this alone will not increase the dealer's sales. In fact, the dealer won't even know if the shirts are appreciated, much less actually worn. Instead, it may be a better idea to mail invitations to local prospects that promise them an attractive MBZ logo T-shirt when they take a test drive. That way, people will actually visit the showroom and the dealer will develop some good leads to follow in the coming months. If the recipients take the trouble to come in and claim their MBZ shirt, they are likely to wear the shirts in public. This provides free advertising for both the Mercedes brand and the local dealership. Many manufacturers like MBZ have cooperative marketing programs, where part of the promotional item costs are paid by the manufacturer. Under this program, you can actually measure the effectiveness of the promo shirt program by linking the program cost to the number of leads generated and eventual car sales.

Another example is that of a promotional T-shirt program to support the grand opening of, for example, a new spa. The spa can simply mail the T-shirts to local residents, which will do little. Alternatively they can invite local residents to participate in a tour of the spa. The promise of a free and attractive spa T-shirt will attract the most likely customers and actually increase sales for the business. These examples demonstrate the difference between wasted free giveaways and effective promotional wear programs.

Promotional apparel can be highly effective for any size of company. Imprinted promotional shirts can be used at the grand opening of a golf course, new gym or hotel. Upscale restaurants can give away logo T-shirts to regular customers or those whose checks exceed a certain dollar amount. Pet stores can give away pet owner T-shirts when a customer buys pet apparel. The applications are endless, and you can actually design a promotional apparel program before you call on a potential new client. With a direct-to-garment printer, you can even print a sample shirt to back up your proposed promo apparel program when visiting a prospect.

There is a host of ideas to consider when designing a promotional wear program for your clients:

- *What to offer:* apparel, mouse pads or other promotional items
- *Apparel styles and colors* currently popular in promotional programs
- *Size mix planning* based on the target audience
- The most *receptive message* to imprint on the shirts or mouse pads
- *Means of delivery,* such as trade shows, showrooms, events, direct mail, courier, or in person through salespeople
- *Related programs* to assure the apparel reaches the most receptive prospects and that the receiving experience is positive
- What kind of receiver will most likely wear the apparel to achieve secondary advertising effects
- How to design the program to avoid "freebie seekers"

Mouse Pads

A digital apparel printer is ideal for printing custom messages on mouse pads. Few people buy mouse pads for themselves. Mouse pads are an ideal promotional product. They are ubiquitously placed on desks; they provide a large space for printing promotional messages; and they are generally less costly than T-shirts. Since digital printing allows for small runs, it's easy to custom design a mouse pad targeted to the receiving party. Suppose you are going to provide 20 mouse pads for a particularly important customer. One idea might be to print all of the internal telephone extension numbers of the company's employees on the mouse pad, with your own number prominently imprinted. Make sure the imprint graphics design is attractive.

Membership in PPAI

If you decide to engage in promotional wear printing and distribution, there are many resources available to help you. Consider becoming a member of PPAI or ASI, or both. These organizations serve the promotional products and advertising specialty industries with professional development programs, publications and trade shows. However, their services are mainly available to dues-paying members.

The Promotional Products Association International (PPAI) is the industry's largest non-profit trade association and has been in operation for more than 100 years. Its 7,500 member firms are mostly from the U.S., but some are from Canada and abroad. PPAI is devoted to the growth of the industry by promoting the power of promotional products, educating the member firms and their professionals, and representing the industry's interests in the legislative arena. It offers a variety of professional development resources that may be of significant help to industry newcomers. There are a number of other benefits as well. Since many of the distributor members are small firms, they provide group insurance, discounted rate plans with various shipping and freight companies, credit service programs, etc. The website, www. ppai.org, also lists the members so that promotional product buyers can find them.

The association holds its gigantic annual members-only trade show, the PPAI Expo, in Las Vegas every January. It is a great place to network and learn about the promotional wear industry. PPAI also offers extensive educational programs during the show.

Membership is organized along the lines of distributor members (68%), supplier members (25%), and others. If you are a direct-to-garment printer, a distributor membership would be the most appropriate since most of your clientele will be end-user corporate customers. Your other potential customers, the distributors of promotional wear who do not have in-house imprinting capabilities, may be uncomfortable placing orders with you since they may perceive you as a competitor. You must be sensitive to their concerns and take informed measures, such as shipping the printed garments to the distributor or using your customer's address as the return address if you are requested to drop-ship. A sure way to please your distributor customer is offering a relabeling service.

Membership in ASI

The Advertising Specialty Institute (ASI) is a for profit membership organization for the promotional product industry. They have more than 28,000 members, classified as suppliers, distributors and decorators. The list of distributor members is available to the public. ASI offers to the distributor members the ESP Online data service which lists the supplier members so that they can find the various promotional items needed to fill corporate orders. Decorator members are primarily screen printers or pad printers who will imprint garments or other products for distributors. Upon joining ASI, you will have access not only to promotional wear blank stock suppliers, but also to a wide variety of promotional items. Since apparel represents the most profitable one-third of the entire industry, you will likely concentrate on promotional wear. In the success stories described in Chapter Four, we learned that 90 percent of Bill's business is imprinted apparel.

ASI holds several regional trade shows in locations such as Las Vegas, Orlando, Dallas, Chicago and New York. These shows are usually well-organized and they offer networking events. If you become a member, you should participate in some of the educational seminars given during the shows. The subjects range from basic promotional product marketing to general management. Both members and public can also subscribe to some of their publications including *Wearables, Uniforms* and *Stitches,* among others. See www.asicentral.com for more details. For direct-to-garment printers, *Wearables* may be a particularly useful magazine.

Membership in Regional Trade Associations

The promotional product industry has regional trade associations, some of which hold smaller trade shows and conventions. The best known of these is the 900-member Specialty Advertising Association of California (SAAC).

SAAC accepts members from other states as well. SAAC's annual dues are modest compared to those of PPAI or ASI, and the dues will entitle you to receive the SAAC monthly publication and attend shows. See www.saac.net for further information.

Some of the other regional trade associations include:

Mid-Atlantic Promotional Products Association (MAPPA)
www.mappa-online.com

Northwest Promotional Marketing Association (NWPMA)
www.nwpma.org

Specialty Advertising Association of Greater New York (SAAGNY)
www.saagny.org

Michigan Promotional Professionals Association (MiPPA)
www.mippa.org

Tri-State Promotional Products Association (TSPPA)
www.tsppa.org

Gold Coast Promotional Products Association (GCPPA)
www.gcppa.org

Promotional Products Association Mid-South (PPAMS)
www.ppams.com

Promotional Products Association Midwest (PPAM)
www.ppam.org

CHAPTER 14

Web Site Operation and Promotion

Although the Internet benefits everyone, it probably is one of the single greatest tools ever conceived for small businesses. Small and home-based businesses can leverage the Internet to a greater degree than can even large businesses. You can control the cost of building, maintaining and marketing it within a budget. There are very few business tools as flexible, cost-effective, and with as much potential to provide limitless information to the customers. That builds the needed credibility for the business.

Building a business and making money with only an Internet presence is not easy. In fact, running an Internet-only business can be both expensive and risky. One of the authors spent several years as the group chair at Tech Coast Angels, the largest angel investor group in the U.S. He reviewed many early-stage technology and Internet companies, invested in some and advised many. Most pure Internet companies find it difficult to grow their businesses because of too much competition due to low barrier to entry. However, many brick-and-mortar companies who made smart and early moves to the Internet benefited enormously. This is a lesson we hope to covey to our readers. Dollar for dollar, there is no medium from which you can get more bang for your marketing buck than a good Web site operation supported by effective Internet marketing. Just don't rely on your Web site to generate *all* your business. A good Web site supplements, not substitutes for old-fashioned sales efforts.

If you have some background in Internet operations, you already know what to do. This chapter is for those who do not. Hiring an Internet marketing specialist could be of significant help. However, you may not have the necessary resources to afford such talent. In any case, it is a good idea to educate yourself in some of the basics of Web site operations and Internet and e-mail marketing. Here are some dos and don'ts.

1. Do build and operate your Web site as soon as possible.
2. Do not attempt to build or maintain Web site yourself unless you are a Web developer.
3. Do make your Web site domain name and your business name the same.
4. Do get a short and easy-to-remember domain name.
6. Do not carry advertisements on your Web site unless they are related to your products.
7. Do make your Web pages clean and professional looking—no flashy graphics.
8. Do not use pop-up windows, particularly exit pop-ups. They are annoying.
9. Do update your Web pages regularly with useful information.
10. Do not use frames in your Web pages.
11. Do work with your developer for key words and search engine optimization.
12. Do monitor your Web site daily.
13. Do respond to all Internet inquiries promptly.
14. Do market your Web site as much as you can.
15. Do tell the truth on your Web site.

Below are some of the basics you can use if you are an Internet novice.

Getting Started and Building the Web Site

1. Get a Web site domain name.
   The domain name is the name of your Web site; it is also used as the Web address. For instance, the IBM Corporation's Web site

domain name is ibm.com. Their URL —the Web address —is www.ibm.com. We recommend strongly that your business name and domain name be the same. If a customer loses your phone number or address, they can look them up in your Web site.

In your search for a domain name, you will find that many attractive, short and easy-to-remember names have already been taken. Because of this, you may really need to do some brainstorming to come up with a name that is easy to spell and easily remembered. If the name also relates to the nature of your business, consider it icing on the cake.

You need to register your domain name with a domain registrar. All registrations are accomplished at Web sites such as www.register. com, www.godaddy.com or www.mydomain.com. To determine availability, go to one of these sites and simply enter the names you have in mind. Domain name suffixes include .com, .net, .info, and .us among others, but it is best to have a .com name since most U.S. customers associate these with businesses. Some domain names available at the time of this writing include TeesByBob.com and SmithPromoShirts.com.

2. Sign Up with a Hosting Company
   Your Web site has to be "hosted" by a Web hosting company unless you want to own an internet server with high speed internet connection. These hosting companies have data centers with banks of Web servers (computers) where the Internet connection is maintained. You can rent slices of these servers from hosting companies. Many of these companies offer free domain name registration when you sign up for their hosting service.

3. Write Your Web Site Content
   The most important thing for you to do is to provide your site content to the Web developer. It's a good idea to visit many different garment decoration Web sites with business models similar to yours. You may even get Web design ideas from these sites for your own. Carefully write out the content you want to see on each page. Use good English and have an editor review your writing

– even if you consider yourself a good writer. Aside from providing basic information about your business, your Web site must also lend itself to credibility. All of the text and content should be very clean and professional looking.

4. Work with a Web Developer

Constructing a basic informational Web site is neither complex nor time-consuming. You can easily find a local Web developer who can help you develop a five- to 10-page basic Web site for a modest cost. There are also companies that offer Web site shells readily available for your use. If you utilize such a developer, all you need to do is to select a shell and theme from the samples they offer. Then, the developer will fill in the blanks with the content you provide. If your time and budget is limited, this may be your best option. Pay particular attention to the look and feel of your site.

Many Web developers are better at writing codes than testing. Although these developers should deliver a clean and bug-free site, you must still go through it yourself to ensure that all features appear as you intended and all links are functional. Once you are satisfied, you can instruct your developer to upload the page files to your server, which will enable you to go live on the World Wide Web.

Marketing Your Web Site

It is estimated that more than 168 million Web sites exist.21 At least 10 million of those are active in the U.S. Therefore, the competition is high, and few people will visit your web site at the beginning. You have two options. First, you can include your Web address in your promotional material, business cards, invoices and packaging, and stationery. This way, you are using it primarily as an informational and credibility-building tool, since the only people visiting your Web site will be those whom you already have made contact with. A second approach is actively marketing your Web site to let the world know that you are open for business, and use it to generate sales leads or generate sales. Here are a few things you can do to monitor and market your site.

1. Search Engine and Directories

   Most people find a Web site by using one of the many Web search
   engines or directories. Best known is Google, and it is by far the
   most important of them all since many other search engines actually rely on Google database. Therefore, your immediate priority in
   Internet marketing is optimizing your Web site for search engine
   optimization (SEO) so that it will rank high on the search results
   pages, particularly in Google.

   For instance, if you enter the key word or search term "direct to
   garment printer" in Google, the results page will look similar to the
   example shown below. The top listing in the yellow shaded area and
   the listings in the right-hand side column are labeled as Sponsored
   Links. These are simply advertisements paid for by the sites' owners.
   This certainly is an option for your Web site, but these pay-per-click
   advertisements are expensive and do not offer much credibility.
   The best spots are high within the left column of the regular search
   results section. In this case, the first listing is "Shopping results,"
   which Google likes to post high on the list. Here, you will see a Fast
   T-jet listed for sale in eBay. The real first place listing is AnaJet.com,
   which appears after the shopping list.

Google Search Results Page: Direct to Garment Printer

You want to be listed high within these search results for as many relevant search terms as possible. So, let's try another search term, "digital apparel printer." The results appear below. Here, you will see again that AnaJet.com is in first place. MelcoJet is listed in second place. When your Web site ranks high on the results page, potential customers are bound to click on your link. Unlike advertisements, visits by those who click your Web site in the search results pages cost you nothing. This kind of site traffic is of vital importance to your business. Realistically, however, it is very difficult to have a high showing consistently on all results pages since there are many Web sites competing. You should at least strive to be listed on the first page of the search results for some of your important key words.

Google Search Results Page: Digital Apparel Printer

After Google, the next most important search engine is Yahoo! Again, if you enter "direct to garment printer" on Yahoo!'s page, you will see AnaJet.com listed in first place just below the sponsored site in the blue shaded area.

Yahoo! Search Results Page: Direct to Garment Printer

Web directories are not as important as search engines, but they are sometimes used by people looking for a particular subject. Below is a listing report taken from the Google directory. There are thousands of directories, and you cannot possibly submit your site information to all of them. It would be best to hire a Web marketing company that will use an automated system to submit your Web site information for a nominal fee to thousands of directories.

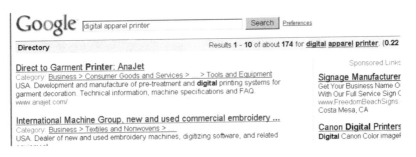

Google Directory Listing: Digital Apparel Printer

AnaJet.com ranks very highly – usually in first, second or third place – in the search results for various reasons. Search engines strive to present first those Web sites that will be most useful to users. In doing so, they apply a myriad of conditions, including the relevance of the site to the search terms, the richness of the site's contents, how frequently the site is updated and the respect commanded by the site as measured by links from other respected sites. As a new and small site, yours may lack many of these attributes at first, but there are many techniques that will enable your site to be ranked fairly and favorably by search engines.

2. Keywords and Search Engine Optimization
   Search engines do not reveal the methods they use to rank Web sites in their listings. As a result, while there are many search engine optimization (SEO) techniques, there are just as many myths. It is important to follow some basic SEO principles as you develop your Web site and during its subsequent revisions, but do not believe all those SEO techniques you find in the internet. Here are some of the most important basic techniques.

   • Create effective meta tags for Title (<title> tag), Description (<description>tag) and Keywords (<keywords> tag). These meta tags are examples of "data describing data," which search engines use to understand, classify and rank your Web site. You should work very closely with your site developer to specify what these tags should be. Do not leave these keywords and meta tag choices to your developer, because your developer is not familiar with your business model as you are. The specification of these keywords is particularly important.

   • Optimize your Web site text copy. Repeat the keywords you want to emphasize several times on each page so that the search engines will recognize that the page relates specifically to each of them. Generally, your primary keywords should appear two to three times for every 100 words. Do not overuse them, since doing so can arouse suspicion within the search engine. However, you may want to use the primary keywords two or three times in the first paragraph of the page. If your Web developer is sufficiently adept at SEO, he can guide you in this effort, but many Web developers are not familiar with SEO. If your budget allows, consider hiring a specialist. Be aware that a good one is hard to find. We found that many expensive "experts" do not deliver.

- Create quality back-links to your Web site. Search engines will prefer your site when many "important" or "authority" Web sites link back to it. This is becoming increasingly important in establishing Google rankings. Find a way to have high traffic sites link to your Web site.

- Create a Google site map. A site map is a list of the pages on your Web site with links to each page. Google site map conforms to Google format specifications, so the Google spider can instantly see and understand your site. For information, visit www.Google.com/webmasters/sitemaps/.

3. Get Listed in Local Directories
   As we indicated earlier, most of your business will come from the local market. Therefore, it is important to become listed in all of your local online directories. You can find your local directories by entering "directory"+"your city name" in a Google search. Submit your Web site and business information to all suitable local directories, including the various online yellow pages. Many people use local directories to find service providers.

4. Monitoring Your Web Site Traffic
   You may want to gauge how much traffic your Web site attracts. You can do this by working with your Web specialist, who can monitor traffic through your server, or you can use the free service offered by Google Analytics. Another way to assess traffic at your Web site is through Alexa ranking. Alexa.com ranks most Web sites based on the traffic they attract. You can download an Alexa toolbar from their site, which will show you your ranking on Alexa. Although it is not entirely accurate, you can get an idea of how much traffic your site generates and whether the traffic is increasing or decreasing.

   If you do not wish to install an Alexa toolbar, simply visit Alexa.com, enter the Web site name, and choose Site Ranking and Go.

Alexa.com Traffic Inquiry Page

In this example, you can see NYtimes.com is 222nd most visited Web site.

Alexa.com Ranking and Traffic Report Page

There are many good books on internet marketing written for small businesses. It will pay handsomely if you read a book or two. We can recommend an easy-to-follow book by Bruce Brown.[22]

Appendix

SPORTSWEAR AND OTHER APPAREL
WHOLESALE SOURCES

Alpha Shirt Company (CA, FL, IN, PA, TX, WA) www.alphashirt.com
  Toll Free: 800-523-4585
  CA: Fresno (P) 800-633-7600 (F) 559-233-2334
  Los Angeles (P) 800-523-4585 (F) 562-802-7761
  FL: St. Petersburg (P) 727-327-3773 (F) 727-323-4802
  IN: Ft. Wayne (P) 260-478-2723 (F) 260-747-5337
  PA: Philadelphia (P) 800-523-4585 (F) 215-673-1497
  TX: Houston (P) 281-277-8311 (F) 281-277-8303
  WA: Seattle (P) 800-523-4585

Americana (CA, CO, OK) www.americanasportswear.com
  Toll Free: 800-473-2802
  CA: Gardena (P) 310-354-1377 (F) 310-354-1386
  CO: Commerce (P) 303-287-7481 (F) 303-287-0640
  OK: Oklahoma (P) 405-557-0004 (F) 405-525-8115

Amtex (IL, GA, TX, MI, CA) www.amtex.com
  Toll Free: 800-421-8337
  IL: Chicago (P) 800-521-0850
  CA: Fresno (P) 800-521-0850
  GA: Duluth (P) 800-521-0850
  TX: Carrollton (P) 800-521-0850
  Stafford (P) 800-521-0850

MI: Plymouth (P) 800-521-0850
KY: Louisville (P) 800-521-0850
MA: Middleboro (P) 800-521-0850
FL: Orlando (P) 800-521-0850
MO: Hazelwood (P) 800-521-0850

Atlanta Tees (GA) www.atlantatees.com
Toll Free: 800-554-1079

Atlantic Coast Cotton (VA) www.accinfo.com
Toll Free: 800-262-5660
VA: (P) 703-753-7000 (F) 703-753-5390

Best Blanks (FL) www.bestblanks.com
Toll Free: 888-431-7385

Bodek and Rhodes (CA, FL, MI, MA, PA) www.bodekandrhodes.com
Toll Free: 800-523-2721
CA: Fresno (P) 559-266-1315
FL: Orlando (P) 407-240-0177
MI: Niles (P) 269-683-3670
MA: Norton (P) 508-285-8566
PA: Philly (P) 215-673-6767

Broder (CA, FL, GA, KY, MI, MO, NY, TX) www.broderbros.com
Toll Free: 800-521-0850

Carolina Made (NC) www.carolinamade.com
Toll Free: 800-222-1409
NC: Charlotte (P) 704-821-6425 (F) 704-821-6752

Commonwealth Cotton (MA) www.commonwealthcotton.com
Toll Free: 800-333-8133
MA: Watertown (P) 617-393-4000 (F) 617-393-3777

Cotton Connection (IL) www.cottonconnection.com
Toll Free: 800-635-1104
IL: Chicago (P) 773-523-0505 (F) 773-523-0554

E.M. T- Shirt Distributors (PR) 787-995-3348

Eva Tees (NY) www.evatees.com
   Toll Free: 800-382-8337
   NY: Long Island City (P) 718-729-1824
   (F) 718-729-1824

Friedman's Activewear (NY) www.friedmansactivewear.com

   Toll Free: 800-872-8671
   NY: New York (P) 212-941-6400 (F) 212-941-6787

Gauss Sales (NY) www.gausssales.com
   Toll Free: 800-828-6775
   NY: Rochester (P) 585-254-3140 (F) 585-254-3160
   Buffalo (P) 716-631-0070 (F) 716-631-2255

Golden Stats T's (CA) www.goldenstatetees.com
   Toll Free: 800-892-8337
   CA: San Jose (P) 408-278-1212
   (F) 408-278-1220

Heritage Sportswear (OH) www.heritagesportswear.com

   Toll Free: 800-537-2222
   OH: Hebron (P) 740-928-7771 (F) 740-928-3223

Imprints Wholesale (CO, KS, NV, WA, WI)
www.imprintswholesale.com
   Toll Free: 800-634-2945
   CO: Denver (P) 303-333-3200 (F) 303-333-7373
   KS: Lenexa (P) 608-845-5600 (F) 800-747-2788
   NV: Las Vegas (P) 702-896-4666 (F) 702-896-4867
   WA: Kent (P) 253-437-1158 (F) 253-437-2031
   WI: Verona (P) 608-845-5600 (F) 800-747-2788

McCreary's Tees (AZ) www.mccrearystees.com
    Toll Free: 800-541-1141
    AZ: Phoenix (P) 602-470-4200

Mission Imprintables (CA) www.missionimprintables.com
    Toll Free: 800-480-0800
    CA: San Diego

NES Clothing Company (MA, NC) www.nesclothing.com
    Toll Free: 800-782-7770
    MA: Middleboro
    NC: Charlotte

One Stop (MI) www.onestopinc.com
    Toll Free: 800-968-7550
    MI: Grand Rapids (P) 616-784-0404
    (F) 800-968-7560

Rivers' End (CA, MN, NV) www.riversendtrading.com
    Toll Free: 800-488-4800
    MN: Hopkins (P) 952-912-2500   (F) 952-912-2525
    NV: Sparks (P) 775-284-7247 (F) 775-284-7262

S&S Activewear, LLC (IL) www.ssactivewear.com
    Toll Free: 800-426-6399
    IL: Bolingbrook

SanMar (FL, NJ, NV, OH, TX, WA) www.sanmar.com
    Toll Free: 800-426-6399
    WA: Seattle (P) 206-727-3200 (F) 206-727-3203
    OH: Cincinnati (P) 800- 426-6399 (F) 800- 828-0554

Sigma Sportswear (MI) www.sigmasportswear.com
    Toll Free: 888-642-0055
    MI: Livonia (F) 313-347-2169

SNS Sales of Nashville (TN) www.snssales.com
Toll Free: 888-257-9800
TN: Nashville (P) 615-251-9900 (F) 615-251-0919

Sol Schultz (OH)
Toll Free: 800-624-2309

Stardust Corporation (KS, LA, OH, WI) www.estardust.com

Toll Free: 800-747-444

Staton Wholesale (CA, FL, IL, TN, TX)
www.statonwholesale.com
Toll Free: 800-888-8888
TX: Dallas (P) 972-448-3000 (F) 972-448-3003
CA: Fullerton (P) 714-680-5422
TN: Memphis (P) 901-362-5554
FL: Orlando (P) 407-855-8301

Sundog International (CA, HI)
Toll Free: 877-48-6364

Thinc Actionwear (OR) www.thincactionwear.com
Toll Free: 800-452-1200
OR: Portland (F) 503-251-1516

TSC Apparel (CA, NC, OH) www.tscapparel.com
Toll Free: 800-289-5400
CA: Fullerton (P) 714-626-6640 (F) 714-871-0375
GA: Acworth (P) 800-553-0021 (F) 800-782-6268
OH: Cincinnati (P) 800-289-5400 (F) 800-248-1069

TSF Sportswear (FL) www.tsfsportswear.com
Toll Free: 800-331-1067
FL: Pompano Beach (P) 954-563-4433
(F) 954-565-5542

Utah Tees and Fleece (UT)
Toll Free: 800-366-5776

Virginia T's (FL, IN, VA) www.virginiats.com
Toll Free: 800-289-8099

Wasatch Tees of Atlanta (GA) www.wasatcht.com
Toll Free: 800-544-9096
Atlanta (P) 404-634-3000 (F) 404-634-1338

Wholesale Printables (VA) www.wholesaleprintables.com
Toll Free: 800-824-7578
VA: Petersburg (P) 804-862-2600 (F) 877-289-8099

Wolf Printables (KY)
Toll Free: 800-882-9653

End Notes and Bibliography

1. The Sovereign Individual, by James Dale Davidson and William Rees-Mogg. Simon & Schuster, 1999.
    Even if you discount many of their unsubstantiated claims and distorted views on economic history, there are many critical lessons in this acclaimed book. Given the steadily accelerating global transition since the twentieth century, the socio-economic changes caused by technological innovations will no longer allow individuals to rely on existing systems to care for them. Individuals must ultimately become self-reliant and proactive, and financially independent in their own way.
2. The Future of Capitalism: How Today's Economic Forces Shape Tomorrow's World, by Lester C. Thurow. Penguin Books, 1997.
    Few economists today understand the glories and limitations of American capitalism better than Professor Lester Thurow of MIT. In this scholarly work, Thurow examines the global, political and economic changes based on the shift to knowledge-based industries. In his view of the future, there is no dominant economic and political power capable of regulating economic activities effectively. While he provides few answers, the ramifications are sufficiently clear. Individuals had better take control of their own destiny and become financially self-reliant.
3. Cashflow Quadrant: Rich Dad's Guide to Financial Freedom,

(Paperback), by Robert T. Kiyosaki and Sharon Lechter. Business Plus, 2000.

This is a follow-up to their widely popular work, Rich Dad, Poor Dad. The authors present compelling reasons why you should become an investor or business owner for more financial freedom and higher upside potential.

4. Millionaire Next Door: The Surprising Secrets of American Wealth by Thomas Stanley and William D. Danko. MJF Books, 2003.

The authors show that, contrary to popular belief, most millionaires of their generation are in fact self-made through hard work and frugal lifestyles. Most millionaires are ordinary folks, not lucky heirs. The book will convince you that it is quite possible for an ordinary person to become a millionaire.

5. The Small Business Economy, For Data Year 2006, A Report to the President. SBA Office of Advocacy, 2007.

6. One Up On Wall Street, by Peter Lynch. Simon & Schuster, 2000.

7. USA Today, March 5, 2008, Technology section. We took the Zazzle story from this report, but did not independently verify the facts.

8. 2007 Decorated Apparel Universe Study. *Impressions* magazine. The most comprehensive decorated apparel industry survey to date.

9. Estimates per unpublished market analysis by the authors.

10. Business Growth Plans, Full Report – May, 2008, SGIA Surveys & Statistics, Specialty Graphic Imaging Association.

11. Direct-to-Garment Ink Jet Printers: State of the Market. Research on Emerging Print Markets, *I. T. Strategies*, January 2007.

12. Advertising Specialty Institute. "Advertising Specialties Sales Reached $19.6 Billion in 2007." Press Release, April 8, 2008.

13. Home-Based Business and Government Regulation. A report by Henry B. R. Beale, for Small Business Administration, Office of Advocacy, 2004.

Although the research was focused on the burden posed by government regulations on small and home-based businesses, you can see some snapshots of the economic status of home-based businesses.

14. The 2006 Estimate of Promotional Products Distributor Sales, PPAI, 2007.

15. "Threading Your Way Through the Labeling Requirements Under the Textile and Wool Acts." Federal Trade Commission, in cooperation with the American Apparel & Footwear Association, May 2005.
Guidelines for labeling requirements in accordance with various Textile and Wool Acts.

16. How to Make a Too Cool T-shirt Quilt, by Andrea T. Funk. Smilie Press, 2005.
Fabulous Tee Shits Quilts, by Caryl Schuetz. Southern Life Publishing Services, 2007.
The Extraordinary T-shirt Quilt: A Scrapbook You Can Sleep Under. CQS Press, 2006.

17. "Photographers and Direct-to-Garment Printers." Market Pulse, *I.T. Strategies*, August 2007.

18. Market Strategies Report – June 2008, SGIA Surveys & Statistics, Specialty Graphic Imaging Association.

19. Selling to Anyone Over the Telephone, by Renee P. Walkup and Sandra McKee. AMACOM, 2005

20. Ultimate Small Business Marketing Guide by James Stephenson and Courtney Thurman. 2nd Ed. (Paperback), Entrepreneur Press, 2007

21. Netcraft estimate, per May 2008 Web Server Survey.

22. How to Use the Internet to Advertise, Promote, and Market Your Business or Web Site, by Bruce C. Brown. Atlantic Publishing Group, Inc. 2006

About the Authors

Chase Roh, Ph.D., is a technologist and entrepreneur. After teaching for several years at the University of Illinois, Urbana, Chase started CR Technology, which developed robotic vision systems. It was sold to Photon Dynamics (Nasdaq: PHTN). His second company, ANAgraph, introduced digital technology to the sign and screen-printing industries. ANAgraph is now a part of OCE, a multi-billion dollar Dutch corporation. In 2004, he co-founded AnaJet to introduce the digital process to apparel printing and has served as its chief executive officer. He is proud to have held only four jobs in his lifetime, each successfully. As a member of Tech Coast Angels, he enjoys investing in and coaching young entrepreneurs.

David A. LaVita, BSC Graduate of the University of Massachusetts, is a sales and business development expert. He has over 25 years of experience in sales and marketing. David has developed and managed distribution channels for both U.S. and international markets for sign making systems, digital printing systems, laser equipment and software products. He has held key management positions in several companies, including ANAgraph. David is a co-founder of AnaJet Inc and serves as one of its senior executives.